Mike Bradw(

Mike Bradwell trained at East 15 Acting School. He played Norman in Mike Leigh's award-winning film *Bleak Moments* and worked as an underwater escapologist and fireater with Hirst's Charivari and as an actor/musician with the Ken Campbell Roadshow.

He founded Hull Truck Theatre Company in 1971 and directed all their shows for ten years, including his own devised plays *Oh What!*, *Bridget's House*, *A Bed of Roses*, *Ooh La La!* and *Still Crazy After All These Years*. Hull Truck toured nationally and internationally and was the first British fringe company to be invited to the National Theatre and to create work for BBC Television.

Mike has directed over forty shows for the Bush Theatre where he was Artistic Director between 1996 and 2007, including *Hard Feelings* by Doug Lucie, *Unsuitable for Adults* by Terry Johnson, *The Fosdyke Sagas* by Bill Tidy and Alan Plater, *Love and Understanding* by Joe Penhall (also at the Long Wharf Theatre, New Haven), *Dogs Barking* by Richard Zajdliz, *Dead Sheep*, *Shang-a-Lang* and *Little Baby Nothing* by Catherine Johnson, *Howie the Rookie* by Mark O'Rowe (also Dublin and Edinburgh Festivals, PS 122 New York, The Magic Theatre, San Francisco, and European tour), *Normal* by Helen Blakeman, *Flamingos* by Jonathan Hall, *Blackbird* by Adam Rapp, *Resident Alien* by Tim Fountain (also New York Theatre Workshop, European and Australian tour), *Airsick* by Emma Frost, *When You Cure Me* by Jack Thorne, *adrenalin…heart* by Georgia Fitch (also Setagaya Theatre Tram, Tokyo), *The Glee Club* by Richard Cameron (also Duchess Theatre, London, Galway Festival and national tour), *The Girl With Red Hair* by Sharman Macdonald (Royal Lyceum, Edinburgh, and Hampstead Theatre), *Crooked* by Catherine Trieschman, and *Pumpgirl* by Abbie Spallen (Edinburgh Festival).

Other work includes *Mrs Gauguin and Mrs Vershinin* by Helen Cooper (Almeida, Riverside and Kampnagel, Hamburg), *Tuesday's Child* by Terry Johnson (Stratford East), *The Cockroach Trilogy* by Alan Williams (national and international tour), *The Dalkey Archive* by Flann O'Brien (Long Wharf Theatre), and productions at the Tricycle Theatre, West Yorkshire Playhouse, King's Head Theatre, Hampstead Theatre, and for the Science Fiction Theatre of Liverpool, the National Theatre of Brent, the Rude Players of Manitoba and the Royal Court Theatre, where he was Associate Director. In addition, Mike has written and directed for film, television and radio, including *The Writing on the Wall*, *Games Without Frontiers*, *Chains of Love*, *Happy Feet* and *I Am A Donut*.

Mike's 2010 production of DC Moore's *The Empire* (Royal Court Theatre, London, and the Drum Theatre, Plymouth) was nominated for Olivier and Evening Standard Awards, and won the TMA Award for Best Touring Production. His book on alternative theatre, *The Reluctant Escapologist*, was nominated for the Sheridan Morley Prize for Theatre Biography, and won the Society for Theatre Research's Theatre Book Prize for 2010.

Also by Mike Bradwell

The Reluctant Escapologist
Adventures in Alternative Theatre

Inventing the Truth

Devising and Directing for the Theatre

Mike Bradwell

NICK HERN BOOKS
London
www.nickhernbooks.co.uk

A Nick Hern Book

Inventing the Truth
first published in Great Britain in 2012
by Nick Hern Books Limited,
14 Larden Road, London W3 7ST

Cover designed by Ned Hoste, 2H
Author photograph by David Harrison (www.davidharrison.info)

Typeset by Nick Hern Books, London
Printed and bound in Great Britain by
Mimeo Ltd, Huntingdon, Cambridgeshire PE29 6XX

A CIP catalogue record for this book
is available from the British Library

ISBN 978 1 84842 153 0

MIX
Paper from
responsible sources
FSC
www.fsc.org   FSC® C019549

Contents

Acknowledgements   vii

Introduction   ix

Making It Up: 1
Techniques Towards Devising a Play

A Bed of Roses by Mike Bradwell   31

Blinding Gloucester: 93
Working with a Text

When You Cure Me by Jack Thorne   137

Acknowledgments

I would like to thank all the actors I have worked with at Hull Truck, the Bush and elsewhere, who have made the whole journey rather than merely reading the brochure.

I would especially like to thank the cast of *A Bed of Roses*: Colin Goddard, Kathy Iddon, Robin Soans, Mia Soteriou, David Threlfall, Heather Tobias and Alan Williams. I would also like to thank Jack Thorne and the brave cast of *When You Cure Me*: Sam Barnett, Danny Bayle, Morven Christie, Lisa McDonald and Gwyneth Strong.

And I would like to thank Philip Thomas, Mike Leigh, East 15 Acting School and Joan Littlewood who taught and inspired me.

M.B.

Introduction

I trained as a director at East 15 Acting School on a directors' course that didn't really exist. East 15 was founded in 1961 by Theatre Workshop actor Margaret Bury in order to pass on Joan Littlewood's principles and techniques to a new generation. Joan had disappeared to Nigeria and the Workshop company had no idea when or if she was going to return. I arrived at the school in October 1967 without a clue about what to expect or what I was doing there. It turned out there were only two directing students, and the notion seemed to be that the pair of us would join in with the first-year acting course, as well as absorbing directing wisdom by stage managing the third-year shows and painting the sets. After that we would play it by ear.

The acting course consisted of classes in Acting, Speech, Laban Movement, *Commedia dell'Arte*, Singing, Fencing and Dramaturgy. Acting tuition was based on Stanislavsky's *An Actor Prepares* and was built around a variety of improvisation exercises, which now might seem commonplace, but back then were regarded as revolutionary and possibly subversive. The majority of the exercises were aimed at either breaking down actors' inhibitions or encouraging spontaneity. Most of them were what are now often categorised as 'theatre sports' or 'theatre games', and were similar to the work pioneered by Bill Gaskill at the Royal Court and Keith Johnstone with Theatre Machine. There were trust exercises and status exercises and exercises involving a fair amount of compulsory and fashionable Sixties groping. There was a propensity towards instant characterisation and the quest for the witty punchline as featured decades later in countless 'improv' clubs and on television in *Whose Line Is It Anyway?* There were also extensive role-playing exercises, in which students spent several weeks living in unrelieved poverty and misery as peasants, or similarly downtrodden unfortunates in meagre hovels constructed in the school orchard. And then, in the third term, Mike Leigh arrived to direct a production of Thomas Dekker's *The Honest Whore*.

Mike used improvisation in a completely different way, seeing it as a way to get to the truth of character and situation. In addition to *The Honest Whore*, Mike devised what he then called 'an improvised play' with third-year students. He uniquely began by creating three-dimensional characters with the actors based on people or combinations of people they knew, and letting the narrative unfold through their interaction. The resulting play, *Individual Fruit Pies*, had an honesty and integrity that I had never seen before, and I decided that I wanted to make the same kind of theatre.

So, in a way, East 15 was a great training.

After East 15 I assisted Mike on his play, *Big Basil*, with the Manchester Youth Theatre, and played Norman in both the theatre and film versions of his *Bleak Moments*. Because it was as an actor that I learnt the devising technique, I still consider it imperative that anyone who wants to direct must have had the experience of acting in a play and appearing on stage. Only by going through the process yourself will you understand what an actor needs.

In 1971 I started my own company, Hull Truck. For the next ten years we toured the country with a series of plays I created through character and improvisation. The first part of this book, 'Making It Up', describes the various techniques I evolved to devise them. I have used my play *A Bed of Roses* to illustrate the process, and the section includes the full text of the production.

A Bed of Roses was devised over twelve weeks in Hull in the summer of 1977 and opened at the Traverse Theatre, Edinburgh, as part of the Edinburgh Festival Fringe. The actors were Colin Goddard, Kathy Iddon, Robin Soans, Mia Soteriou, David Threlfall, Heather Tobias and Alan Williams.

After Hull Truck I worked as a freelance director in theatre, film and television. I was Artistic Director of the Bush Theatre in London from 1996 to 2007.The second part of the book, 'Blinding Gloucester', shows how I have adapted the character-building techniques used in devised plays for work on written texts. To illuminate the process I have used Jack Thorne's play *When You Cure Me*, which I directed at the Bush in 2005. The section also includes the text of the play.

There are as many ways to direct a play as there are directors. There are no hard-and-fast rules and there is no mysterious alchemical process. There is no Philosopher's Stone.

Using Mike Leigh's devising techniques will not make you a great director any more than borrowing Harold Pinter's typewriter will turn you into a great playwright.

There are as many different ways to prepare for a performance as there are actors. Actors, like politicians, are magpies. They nick stuff from everywhere and use what they need. The director's job is to coax them to give the most truthful performances they can. Personally, I have found that working organically through character and subtext is the most likely way to make this happen. I don't profess to have a method and, also being a magpie, I freely confess to nicking stuff from everywhere – but there are techniques that I frequently return to.

These you will find in this book.

Having said that, it's not a matter of how you do it; it's more what the punters experience when they watch what you do with it.

Making It Up

Techniques Towards Devising a Play

There are as many ways of devising plays as there are directors, actors and companies that devise them.

It is equally true that every time I have devised a play for stage or television my working method has changed depending on the project, the actors, the time available for rehearsal and the nature of the story I find myself telling. So what follows is a rough guide, if you like, to how I do it and a general outline of the basic principles involved in creating a play through improvisation.

Improvised Plays

As far as I am concerned, there are two kinds of improvised play – those that start out with me having a general idea of the territory I want to explore and those where I haven't a clue what is going to happen. For example, the television play I devised for the BBC in 1980, *Games Without Frontiers*, was always going to be set on the midnight ferry between Harwich and the Hook of Holland, and I would imagine that Mike Leigh had Gilbert and Sullivan firmly in mind when he embarked on *Topsy-Turvy*.

On the other hand, *A Bed of Roses*, the play I am focusing on here, falls into the latter category, in as much as I had absolutely no idea whatsoever what the story would turn out to be. I only knew that it probably would be set in Hull because we were going to rehearse it in Hull. One would reasonably imagine that a journey into the complete unknown would engender more fear in the heart of the director than a play with even the most rudimentary predetermined theme, but, in truth, one always sets out with the same mixture of trepidation, exhilaration and abject terror.

In practice, the length of rehearsal time is a major factor in determining how much pre-planning I do. With the major Hull Truck plays I allowed myself twelve weeks' rehearsal, so I could start with little more than a glimmer of an idea. With the television plays I had between four and six weeks, so had to go into rehearsals with a certain amount of knowledge as to what the final tale might be. Either way, the story really begins with the casting.

Auditions and Casting Workshops

In the early days of Hull Truck I worked with pretty much anybody who would turn up, but even then I was aware that I was looking for actors and performers with humour, imagination and an ability to tell the truth.

They had to have a gift for observation and a willingness to set out into the unknown. They had to trust the working method, or it wouldn't work; and they had to realise that it wasn't about them. There are no star parts. It is a collective process. I recruited the later companies through a series of interviews and workshops.

After advertising in *The Stage* and *Time Out*, I sifted the hundreds of replies looking for people who seemed on paper to have the right attitude towards the work. After a couple of rounds of interviews, during which I chatted to the actors about their backgrounds and anything other than theatre, I set up a series of workshops. The actors had to arrive having created a character based on somebody they knew, who could be living alone in Hull or London or Manchester or wherever the workshop was taking place. The basic rule was that the character had to be roughly the same age, the same gender and the same pigmentation as they were. And not an actor. During the course of the day I would take them through an abbreviated version of the character-building process, allowing them time to work alone and allowing me time to observe how well they could concentrate. The workshop culminated in a group improvisation.

During the course of the day I had introduced the notion that each of these characters had seen an advert in *Time Out* inviting them to an introductory evening for a Lonely Hearts Club and decided to go along. The actors then went out in character through the streets of Hull or London or Manchester or wherever, and when they came back, the workshop space had become the Lonely Hearts Club. One of my company played the part of the organiser, introducing the characters to each other. There was a bar and dancing. The purpose was to see who could sustain character truthfully without either showing off or manufacturing some kind of melodramatic event.

The workshops taught me who I thought could do it and who I thought had the imagination to come up with something truthful and interesting. The actual selection of actors is the first determining factor in the shape of the play-to-be.

I am, of course, stating the bleeding obvious, but if I choose three male actors and three female actors there is a strong possibility that the play might be about three couples. This was the case with *A Bed of Roses*, the play I'm using as an example in this chapter.

If I were to choose two actors in their fifties, two in their thirties and two in their twenties, it's a fair bet that the final play might involve either family or generational conflict. If I have a more specific idea or theme in mind I will select actors that I think will be capable of coming up with characters who will fit into the general parameters of the tale I am going to tell. For example, I made a television piece for Channel Four called *Chains of Love* which I knew was going to be set at an Ann Summers party where women would buy sex aids. Accordingly, I cast six women who would create characters who could possibly go to such an event. If I wanted to set a play in Belfast I would cast actors who came from there or who at least had a working acquaintance with the city and the lives of its people.

Another factor in casting is class. This is not to say that actors are not capable of playing characters from different strata of society than the ones they grew up in, but if I were to make a play about, say, ex-public schoolboys, I would need actors with at least a passing knowledge of the psychological consequences of such an education.

Choosing the Characters

Before rehearsals start I ask the actors to come up with a list of people they know or that they have met, who they may be interested in playing. This is not to say that they are going to be asked to impersonate someone they know, but rather the selected character provides a target to aim at. I may provide them with brief guidelines – in the initial stages of *A Bed of Roses*, I asked Robin Soans and David Threlfall to choose characters involved in communication in some way – or I might leave the choice entirely to them. I begin working with each actor individually, in conditions of total secrecy. This is not for any wanky, holy or mysteriously conspiratorial purpose; it is totally central to the whole process that each actor only finds out information about other characters when organically necessary. Put in most simple terms: if you were to find out that you are playing a policeman and someone else is playing a villain, you would make a value judgement about what your possible relationship with the other character might be. If the actors talk to each other about who they are playing, it is inevitable that each of them will try to second-guess what the play might be about and their character's role in it. This can lead – and indeed has – to an actor trying to gear the improvisations in a particular direction to suit his imagined scenario for his character. Mike Leigh used to hang a wartime poster on the rehearsal room wall that read 'CARELESS TALK COSTS LIVES'. And he meant it.

For the first few days I sit with each actor individually and we talk about the people on their list.

This is a time for storytelling. If an actor has a list of six people we will discuss six individual stories. In preparation for *A Bed of Roses*, Robin Soans was interested in, amongst others, a visionary architect, a Vietnam War photographer and a vicar. David Threlfall came up with either someone who worked in advertising/marketing or was a journalist who told jokes. It is not the profession of the character that is most interesting; it's the psychological journey of how they got to be who they are. Over several days we excavate their lives and find out what makes them tick, why they behave like they do. I am looking for something that excites the actor and the idiosyncratic kind of detail that I think might serve the drama, whatever that might turn out to be. If I have six actors and they each have brought six characters to the table, I am now juggling thirty-six lives and looking for possible connections and potential relationships and conflicts between them. The secret is not to panic and go for the first, easiest or most obvious choice; you have to trust your intuition and see where it leads you. Always go for what you find dangerous or unpredictable.

In the case of *A Bed of Roses*, the first choice I made was to go with Robin's vicar. This was partly because I was interested in examining the nature of vicaring, but mostly because of the duplicitous qualities of the man Robin wanted to base his vicar on. I also encouraged Kathy Iddon to develop one of her characters who had spent time doing Voluntary Service Overseas, as I felt that this would in some way connect with Robin's vicar story. These sort of decisions influence the choices I make about the characters that the other actors will create. I do not have a plot or even a plan in mind, but I am looking for the potential for future interaction between them. The next step is to build the characters we have selected. We start by creating life histories.

Life Histories

Again working with each actor individually and in secret, we create biographies for our by now fictitious characters in minute detail. I begin with the character's parents, grandparents and the first house they lived in. I take them through their earliest memories, school days, puberty and adolescence from the moment they were born up to the time of the play. We always work chronologically. Each new piece of information feeds into the next. I concentrate on everything from education, religion, financial situation, morality and sexuality, to their interests in art, literature, popular culture and eating habits. We discuss everything from childhood illness to ghosts, nicknames and bullying. We explore the character's fantasies and ambitions and their secrets. These sessions provide the bedrock on which the characters are built, and in addition provide me with potential material to be explored in the final play, as well as material for the actors to explore in future improvisations.

Throughout these discussions the actor must always refer to his character in the third person: '*His* best friend at primary school was Eric Boocock.' '*She* won a *Blue Peter* badge for saving a Bedlington Terrier from drowning.' This forces the actor to maintain a degree of objectivity about the character. They are playing a part. We are rehearsing a play. This is neither psychodrama nor behavioural therapy.

At the same time as we are creating background histories, the actors will often be engaged in character research. In rehearsals for *A Bed of Roses*, Robin Soans spent weeks finding out about the training involved in becoming a vicar and interviewing most of the clergy in Hull about their pastoral duties. His discovery that most of the churches were kept locked eventually provided the idea for the character's sermon, 'Who is your house open to?' David Threlfall went to work at the *Hull Daily Mail*. An actor playing someone who works in a factory should spend time discovering what it is like to work in a factory. The director, as part of the rehearsal process, should devise exercises to explore the daily workplace rhythms of the character's chosen profession and what it entails, be he either a barrister or a fish-gutter.

Visualisation and Solo Exercises

The next step involves a series of visualisation exercises. The actors sit comfortably and close their eyes while I take them on imaginary journeys through aspects of their life history. I ask them to imagine the first house they lived in, their parents, their journey to school, their first job, their first sexual experience, a wedding or a funeral the character has attended. The list is endless and varies with every character and every project. The idea is that they play the movie of the scene in their head. The purpose is to enable them to begin to think themselves *into* character as opposed to thinking *about* the character. Character is biography in action.

The final visualisation exercise involves the actor creating the room in which the character spends most time alone. We then create a version of that room in the rehearsal space. Part of the stage manager's job when working on a devised play is to provide a comprehensive kit of chairs, tables, beds, sofas, etc., with which we can create character environments. I also use hospital screens to delineate areas and the dimensions of the space. I then set up the circumstances in which the character finds him or herself in this particular room at this particular time on this particular day: She has come back from work. She has a cold. She is going to meet her boyfriend. She doesn't like him much.

The actor's job is to inhabit that room in character. They have to begin to think how the character might think. Again, the secret for the actor is just to let things happen and resist the temptation to be interesting, impressive or entertaining. It's also important to dissuade them from making imaginary telephone calls to other imaginary characters or invent mimed business. As we used to say in Hull Truck, 'When in doubt, do nowt.'

The purpose of this solo work is twofold. It gives the actor the opportunity to work on aspects of characterisation in isolation, without the pressure of having to interact with other characters. As part of the process we spend time working on the physicality of the character. Are they light or are they heavy? Fast or slow? Direct or indirect? How is their physicality determined by their job, environment, social status? It's also an opportunity to experiment vocally with accent, timbre, etc.

By now the actor will also have assembled a rehearsal costume – a simple change of clothing which they wear when in character. It could involve wearing a suit, or a different length skirt, different shoes and different make-up. How do they present themselves to the world?

The lone improvisations also provide material for me as a writer/deviser. After each improvisation I question the actors about what they did and felt, and their answers can often determine the direction in which I decide to take their characters. We discuss each character's hopes and fantasies and these revelations will often give me the basis for the subsequent plot. For example, in an earlier play, *The Knowledge*, I discovered that one of the characters was a compulsive liar. The final play revolved around her mendacity.

We repeat the solo improvisations over a number of days, working chronologically and reinventing the background scenario each day so as to analyse how the character's behaviour changes with variations of mood and circumstance. Eventually we take the characters out for a walk.

The actor, in costume, sets out with a given set of circumstances and completes a task in character. It can be as simple as buying a newspaper or a lottery ticket; it can be going to the park and feeding the ducks; but the purpose of the exercise is for the character to exist in, and interact with, the real world. When Robin Soans as Alex, the vicar, walked round Hull in character and costume he discovered that he was treated in a completely different way by members of the public. They either greeted him warmly or quickly crossed the road. He discovered that his entire bearing changed when he wore the dog collar. Mia Soteriou had created a semi-vagrant character called Mel, who was based on someone she had seen busking in Oxford. Mel indulged in a little light shoplifting so I sent Mia out in character to do some robbing, having first tipped off the shopowner that she was coming. Not only did she successfully nick stuff from the forewarned bookshop, she got away with shoplifting from several innocent stores as well.

Character Interaction

So we now have a number of characters who exist in isolation with developed backgrounds and life histories, and actors who have now reached a stage where they can get into character convincingly. During the process so far I have been looking for clues as to which character should interact with which. The next job is to begin to explore the potential relationships between them. Again, there are a number of ways of going about this. The way I put together *A Bed of Roses* illustrates several of them.

David Threlfall's character Philip had moved to Beverley with his parents and worked as a trainee journalist on the local Hull newspaper, compiling the questions for the quiz page and reporting on dog shows. In background discussions we had decided that Philip was a joker who communicated almost exclusively in funny voices. Heather Tobias had created Julie, a prim secretary who lived in Belfast. I determined that the two characters should meet. Together, Heather and I created the circumstances in which Julie found herself moving to Hull to escape from a broken relationship. In Hull Julie applied for a number of secretarial posts. One of them was for the *Hull Daily Mail*. There she encountered Philip. I set up a series of improvisations in which they saw each other from a distance walking round town, and then in the rehearsal room I set up a scene where they met for the first time in a coffee bar at lunchtime. The initial meeting was unspectacular, but she thought he was funny and he quite fancied her, so we had the basis for exploring a relationship between them. The first improvisations where people meet are notoriously loaded, as the actors know what they are in the improvisation for (to meet each other), and the results are obviously predictable. There is also a tendency for the actors to come out with *all* the biographical detail they have been preparing for the previous three weeks. The Philip and Julie relationship was initiated through a naturalistic improvisation.

The relationship between Alex, the vicar, and Meg (Kathy Iddon) was arrived at by different means. Kathy had decided that Meg had spent time doing VSO in Africa after leaving university. I nudged Robin in the same direction, so Alex went off to Africa as well. Rather than setting up jungle improvisations, we sat around the table and discussed how they met and how their relationship developed. We would, however, set up key scenes in their story. For example, we would improvise their first date together. I would then talk to the actors individually (and confidentially) about what they thought had happened in the scene. Meg wanted Alex to kiss her. Alex thought she didn't want to be kissed. We would then discuss what happened next until we arrived at a point that required a naturalistic improvisation to provide the actors with an actual memory rather than a constructed event. I knew that Alex planned to ask Meg to marry him. Meg, of course, had no idea that this was going to happen, so the reaction she had when it happened in an improvisation was far more grounded than if the proposal had happened in a discussion round the table. We slowly moved the relationship forward, discussing their return to England, their wedding, their sex life and their lives together in various parishes until we located them ten years later in 1977 – the time of the play – living in Hull in a loveless marriage. We worked on a year at a time, devoting one day to each year using both discussions and naturalistic improvisations in the rehearsal room and on location.

The Philip and Julie story was explored in the same way, but more often in naturalistic improvisation because the time frame of their relationship stretched over eighteen months rather than ten years. An important aspect of their tale was Julie's reluctance to sleep with Philip. We constructed a series of improvisations and exercises to emphasise Philip's frustration. Eventually he took her away for an idyllic weekend at a B&B in Robin Hood's Bay and ended up reluctantly getting engaged. So in 1977 they were living in Hull, Philip still at home with his parents, and planning their wedding.

The investigation of a character's sexual history is an integral – if delicate – part of the process. I am not convinced that it is either possible or desirable to have an improvised fuck, so there are several ways to approach the matter. The first is to set up a visualisation exercise, which involves the actor imagining the encounter. The second is by discussion, making sure to check each of the participant's individual version of the event separately and secretly – e.g. Philip thought it was great, Julie thought it was crap.

The third is to use an exercise I nicked off Mike Leigh, who adapted it from Jimmy Roose-Evans, who nicked it off Lee Strasberg.

In my version the actors sit facing each other with their hands on the table in front of them. They are given a set of circumstances. It could be, for example, that they are sharing a room in a B&B in Robin Hood's Bay. They focus their character into their hands and let the hands play out the story. One person will approach the other and the other will join in or draw back. One will close up into a fist; the other will stroke their partner's hand. What you get is a representation of the physicality of the relationship in the chosen circumstances, but told abstractly. You then discuss with the actors the implications of the story that has been played out by their hands. It's not an exercise about miming a shag; it's an exercise that can illuminate intimate aspects of a relationship that cannot be explored with a physical improvisation.

Alan Williams had created a character called Trevor, who was a borderline lunatic and part-time criminal. He claimed to have a metal plate in his head, which enabled him to received messages from Johnny Cash and dead people. He also dabbled in amateur Satanism. Kathy Iddon had decided from her research into vicars' wives that one of Meg's pastoral duties was visiting prisoners in jail. Alan created a scenario in which Trevor went house-breaking. I decided that he got caught. He got six months in Hull prison. I set up a series of improvisations in which Meg visited Trevor in prison. Meg, way out of her depth, patronised Trevor, but he didn't notice. Despite the fact that they had nothing in common whatsoever, they forged a bond together, and Meg determined to see Trevor after his release to see how he was getting on.

Mia Soteriou's vagrant character Mel was bumming around the country aimlessly. Late one night she gets a lift to Hull and ends up being dropped at the railway station. Trevor hangs around the station late at night. They meet up and Mel, having nowhere to crash, goes back to Trevor's bedsit. She stays, and a weird non-sexual relationship develops between them, based on mutual need, loneliness and petty crime. I set up this encounter as an improvisation on location. We dropped Mia at Selby Fork, and she hitched back to Hull in character. Her instructions were to get to the station when she arrived, as that was the only place where you could get a cup of tea at that time of night. She did not know who she was going to meet or indeed if she was going to meet anybody. Alan, as Trevor waiting at the station, did not know that Mia was going to turn up. Obviously the whole encounter was manufactured and the actors inevitably felt beholden to interact in some way, but the location and circumstance in which the characters met, and the seedy nighthawks in the Hull Station diner, permeated their entire relationship and gave it a quality that I don't

13

think would have been achieved if the improvisation had taken place in the rehearsal room.

We now had the six central characters from *A Bed of Roses* living in Hull at the same time and all interacting with each other. The play would eventually chronicle the disintegration of their relationships.

There are other ways of bringing characters together.

Working on *Ooh La La!* – an earlier play set on a university campus – I realised that the characters created by actors John Blanchard and Bridget Ashburn would work as father and daughter. Accordingly, we set out creating a joint background, reinforced by naturalistic improvisation at various points in their common history. Importantly, Bridget's character, Monica, was only ever given the information that her father Tony would have shared with her and vice versa. The characters kept their own secrets. Thus Monica's discovery of the truth behind the circumstances of her mother's death became a central plotline in the eventual play.

Occasionally it becomes necessary to realign the character backgrounds in order to explore a particular relationship.

In my play *Oh What!*, actors Cass Patton and Rachel Bell had created two diametrically opposed characters, Mandy and Celia. As part of the backstory I had decided that, several years before the play took place, they had been students together living on the same floor in a halls of residence. After a series of perfunctory improvised encounters it became obvious that the characters couldn't stand each other. There was absolutely no likelihood of them staying in touch after university and even any contrived future meeting seemed unlikely. The only way to keep the characters joined at the hip despite their mutual animosity was to make them sisters. Accordingly we realigned their biographies, creating a shared background, parents and family. In the final play, Mandy, who lives in London and works as a fashionista at *Cosmopolitan* magazine, visits pregnant hippy Celia in her country cottage, having been dispatched by their father to sort out Celia's life. The motor for the piece was the clash between their opposing philosophies and lifestyles.

Telling the Story

The next part of the devising process is to set up the improvisations on which the play will be based.

At this stage in the proceedings I usually have an indication of the direction in which I think the play might go. In the case of *A Bed of Roses* I had three couples whose relationships were in flux, and I wanted to see where they would end up. I also knew that Alex and Meg, with their Christian zeal, would end up becoming involved with all of them.

Improvisations move forward consecutively, and the results of each improvisation suggest which aspects of the story to explore next.

In the Philip and Julie story, Julie is pushing ahead with plans for the wedding and Philip is reluctantly going along with them. We improvised a number of scenes in which Philip became increasingly less enthusiastic about Julie's plans and was unwilling to name the day. I then set up a scenario in which Julie had arranged to meet Philip in a bar after work so that they could go house-hunting. Heather, playing Julie, had previously visited several bona fide estate agents in character and provided herself with a sheaf of property details. Unbeknown to Julie, Philip arrived in the bar an hour early and met up with his infantile hairdresser mate, Wayne (Colin Goddard). By the time she arrived they were pissed and fooling about. Julie eventually persuaded Philip to go house-hunting with her after a vague promise of sex, but the evening ended in tears.

After each improvisation I talked to the actors individually and monitored what had happened between them, what the subtext of the scene was and what direction they felt the characters were going in. After the 'house-hunting' improvisation, Heather felt that Julie would break off the engagement. This was a development that it would have been impossible to foresee, but I decided to go along with it to see where it would lead. Accordingly, I set up a phone-call improvisation in which Julie dumps Philip. She was surprised when Philip readily agreed to call the whole thing off. I then worked with Philip and Julie on their individual reactions to the break-up. Julie was upset and angry and in her anger decided to stop taking the pill. She realised that she manufactured the split in an attempt to force Philip to commit. Her strategy had backfired, but she is too proud to call Philip and make up. Philip was initially happy about the situation and could spend more time (in more improvisations) getting drunk with Wayne. But eventually he became lonely and, wanting some sex, called Julie up and the relationship was back on again. This led to the next naturalistic improvisation, which found them fooling about in bed together after they had made up. Philip tried to have sex but Julie stopped him, as she was no longer on the pill. She pretended to have forgotten to take it. Philip got angry. They had a row. Philip had an asthma attack. Then they made up.

We continued exploring the relationship as Julie continued to plan the wedding and the accommodation of the legion of her Northern Irish relatives who would be descending on Hull for the great day. There were more rows, more asthma attacks. It's on, then it's off again, then it's on again. Where this was, of course, all heading was the improvisation we'd been gearing up to for several weeks in which Philip and Julie finally go round to their parish priest to arrange the wedding and meet Alex and Meg. The dramatic irony in the scene is that we have Alex, a pompous bully in a failed marriage with Meg, giving advice on the nature of love and fidelity to Philip, an immature bully in a doomed relationship with Julie.

As well as Philip and Julie's story, I was simultaneously working on the parallel stories of Alex and Meg, and Trevor and Mel.

Key improvisations included:

- Trevor goes round for dinner with Alex and Meg when he leaves prison.
- Trevor experiments with rudimentary black magic.
- Mel and Trevor try to sell broken transistor radios at Hull Market.
- Mel meets Meg.
- Alex and Meg's relationship deteriorates.
- Alex goes round to confront Trevor about black magic and Trevor throws him out.
- Alex bans Meg from seeing Trevor.
- Meg visits Trevor again.
- Trevor freaks out and tells Mel how the voices he hears in his head are the Klansmen from Heaven telling him to kill all the blacks.
- Mel runs away.
- And Wayne gets his offstage girlfriend Pam pregnant.

The process continues until I feel the tale has been told and I have enough material from which to make the play. It is a purely intuitive decision. The amount of time this takes is of course dependent on the amount of rehearsal time I have got. In a twelve-week rehearsal period I would usually spend two-thirds of the time on background character work and improvisation, and the last third on constructing and rehearsing the final play. For shorter rehearsal periods the ratio would differ.

During the improvisations I lurk in a corner and take brief notes on what has happened. These are mainly as an aid towards the post-improvisation discussions – e.g. 'What did Julie feel when Philip said "I suppose a shag's out of the question?"?' – but they also provide an indication of key moments in the storytelling. I have at various times experimented with taping improvisations, especially when I have had a short rehearsal period or there are several conversations going on at once, but I generally find this to be more of a hindrance than a help. It is a mistake to get bogged down with the particular, rather than homing in on the essence of a situation. With these notes as a rough guide I go away and write the scenario for the play.

Writing the Scenario

What I come back with is a simple structure, often providing only a brief indication of what might happen in each scene. The scenario may chronologically follow the events explored over the improvisation period, but equally it could include new scenes suggested to me by the direction of the improvisations, or scenes that are distillations of many improvisations. The scenario also dictates the time signature of the piece. It is possible that a twelve-week rehearsal period will engender a play in which the action takes place over several months. Such was the case with *A Bed of Roses,* which began on the eighteenth Sunday after Trinity and ended on Advent Sunday. It is equally possible that that the action of the play will take place on a single evening, as with Mike Leigh's *Abigail's Party.*

The scenario for *A Bed of Roses* went something like this:

- Alex's first sermon: 'Who is your house open to?'
- Meg visits Trevor in prison where she feeds him fig rolls.
- Philip and Wayne get pissed in a bar, and discuss women and Julie.
- Trevor goes to supper with Meg and Alex at the vicarage.
- Julie arrives in the bar to meet Philip and Wayne. She wants to view houses.
- Trevor and Mel try to fix a broken radio. They row.
- Philip and Wayne speak on the phone. Philip's engagement is off.
- Trevor and Mel attempt to conjure demons. Mel burns a Bible.
- Meg tells Alex about Mel and Trevor's black magic rituals.
- Philip and Julie are in bed. They row and Philip has an asthma attack.
- Alex goes to see Trevor and Mel. Trevor throws him out.

Interval

- Trevor and Mel play the card game 'Cheat' and go to bed.
- Julie plans the wedding. Philip wants to work on a kibbutz.
- Julie and Philip go to see Alex and Meg to discuss the wedding. Philip takes the piss.
- Julie and Philip row in the car. He has an asthma attack. She gives in.
- Meg visits Trevor and Mel. She thinks they are lovers.

- Trevor tells Mel about killing blacks and JFK. Mel splits.
- Meg tells Alex about seeing Trevor. Alex goes to church.
- Philip and Wayne speak on the phone. Wayne is getting married.
- In the pulpit Alex publishes Julie and Philip's wedding banns.
- Alex's second sermon: 'A new commitment to Christ.'

From this scenario I now begin to structure the actual scenes in the play. Again, I will illustrate the several ways of approaching this with scenes from *A Bed of Roses*.

Methods of Scene Construction

1) Conventional Scripting

Alex's two sermons that bookend the play were written last and were actually scripted. Robin and I discussed Alex's frame of mind before and after the events of the play took place, and Robin went off and wrote the sermons in character.

'Who is your house open to?' was inspired by Robin's discovery that all the churches in Hull were kept locked.

> So I made a few enquiries and I always got the same answer: 'We can't afford a verger.' 'I see – what do you need a verger for?' 'Isn't it obvious?' they would reply. 'It's to keep out the thieves, the tramps, the drunks and the hooligans.' So who is your house open to? As Christians, I mean. As Christians would you really welcome strangers in here – or tramps – niggers, Krauts, wops, Eyeties, Jews? I mean, Jews? – Where the whole thing began? In the second lesson today we heard the parable of the hundred sheep. Now, God trusted the ninety and nine – he went after the hundredth sheep, the stray sheep, the tramp, the drunk and the hooligan. So it

> seems, does it not, that most of our churches specifically
> bar their doors to keep out the very people who God is
> most anxious should come in. Actually, did you ever
> hear anything so bloody stupid?

The sermon both introduces Alex's character and his liberal Christian ethics, and at the same time sets up the theme of the play. In the last sermon, Alex, who by now has realised that his marriage to Meg is beyond redemption and who has had a brick thrown through his window by Mel, self-importantly and hypocritically casts himself in the role of a Christian martyr, equating his 'suffering' to that of Dr Sheila Cassidy, the aid worker who was tortured by Chilean fascists. He has in fact learnt nothing.

> We are bound to suffer setbacks, and when the
> electrodes are strapped to our bodies, it is time for self-
> examination certainly, but it is no time for the
> faint-hearted. When we reach the breaking point it is
> merely a platform for a new assault on the evils around
> us, time for a new commitment to Christ.

In this case, the material was generated by events discovered through improvisation, but the actual script was tailored not only to communicate Alex's state of mind and self-regard, but also to serve the dramatic structure of the play.

2) Distillation

Meg's visit to Trevor in prison was a distillation of a number of prison-visit improvisations over several weeks. Meg had always arrived with fig rolls, cans of cherryade and cigarettes, and nervously forced them on Trevor to such an extent that he had previously gone down with the shits. Trevor had remained monosyllabic through most of the visits, and Meg had to work hard to keep him engaged in conversation. Over the weeks, Trevor had grown to trust her despite her middle-class demeanour. He had told her about his family and his life before prison. It was important that the final scene reflected this relationship but also introduced the audience to the characters and set up the plot. To achieve this I revisited an improvisation set just before Trevor's release, but gave the actors specific objectives and circumstances. Meg's objective was to rehabilitate Trevor and gather him into the flock – the hundredth sheep. She invited him round to supper at the vicarage with Alex, enlisted him to help with the Christmas decorations, tried to get him to join the church football team, and suggested he became a member of the Men's Fellowship. Trevor's objective was to resist most of these suggestions. His rejection of the invitation to join the football team meant that Trevor could tell Meg (and the audience) about his childhood accident resulting in a four-year stay in hospital and a metal plate in his head. He also emphatically refused the proffered fig rolls. We repeated the improvisation several times, refining the detail each time to illuminate all the nuances of their relationship. In the final version Trevor grudgingly agrees to go round to the vicarage for supper on the Monday after his release (who is your house open to?). The scene contains the essence of the original improvisations, but has shape and dramatic function arrived at organically with the actors. The improvisations each lasted half an hour, the duration of an actual prison visit. The scene lasted four minutes.

3) Scripting Plus Distillation

Scenes with Philip and Wayne in the bar were arrived at partially by the distillation process and partly by scripting.

The two actors had worked for weeks on the characters' shared sense of humour and the nature of their 'double act'. Wayne and Philip were a pair of jokers who spoke almost exclusively in funny voices and routines from TV comedy shows. They had spent a lot of time watching *Monty Python*, *The Goodies*, *Some Mothers Do Have 'Em* and daytime kids' shows, and the actors did likewise. They could move from Tommy Cooper to Morecambe and Wise and from Bruce Forsyth to *Blue Peter* without pausing for breath. In one of the many bar-room improvisations, Philip and Wayne remembered a night out when they had pulled a couple of girls and got them drunk. Philip's girl had passed out – 'comatose interruptus' – and Wayne's had been sick in his hairdressing salon. In another bar impro the pair had talked disparagingly about Philip's engagement to Julie.

We constructed the final bar scene using both these story elements, but with the added condition that Philip was waiting for Julie as they were supposed to be going house-hunting. The 'lads' night out' tale was told as John Cleese and Frank Spencer, and the Julie story was told as a series of Irish jokes.

WAYNE. How is Julie then?

PHILIP. Oh, she's thick. Eh, listen, she went into the building society yesterday to put some of my money in, and she said to the bloke behind the counter. (*Bad Belfast accent.*) 'Eh, youse!!'

WAYNE (*even worse Belfast accent*). 'Eh, youse!!'

PHILIP. 'Eh, youse, Seamus, you I want to put some of me and my fiancé's money in here, right.' So he said, 'Certainly, madam, can you identify yourself?' So she put her hand in her handbag, pulls out a mirror and says, 'Oh yes, I tink that's me all right!'

WAYNE. She's so thick she thought Sheffield Wednesday was a public holiday.

PHILIP. She thought Muffin the Mule was a sexual offence.

WAYNE. She thought Sherlock Holmes was a block of flats.

PHILIP. She threatened to sue the baker for forging her signature on the hot-cross buns.

We collectively wrote the jokes.

4) Further Improvisation

The scene where Trevor goes to supper at the vicarage illustrates another version of the structuring process.

Initially we repeated the original improvisation. Trevor came round bringing a gift of Newcastle Brown Ale. Meg and Alex tried very, very hard to be friendly but in fact were middle class and patronising. Meg as usual talked incessantly. They ate roast chicken. Alex suggested Trevor pick up his chicken bone. The meal was tense and everyone was relieved when it was over. The scene just about worked dramatically, but there was clearly something missing.

As usual, after the improvisation I discussed what had happened in the scene with the actors individually. What the discussion revealed was the true level of antagonism between Alex and Meg, whereas the scene only revealed the tension between the characters when they were on their best behaviour. I set up a completely new improvisation that started with Trevor's departure and in which Meg and Alex analyse the events of the evening, and bicker about each other's behaviour towards him. I thought this was more revealing than the original. The new scene gave an insight into the state of Alex and Meg's marriage, and their true attitudes towards Trevor, and so became the basis for the final version.

> MEG. Did you like him?
>
> ALEX. Yes, very much.
>
> MEG. What do you mean, 'very much'?
>
> ALEX. Very much.
>
> MEG. You can't like him very much; you don't know him very well.
>
> ALEX. You don't keep your mouth shut very often, but it's very pleasant when you do.
>
> MEG. I wonder what he thought of us?
>
> ALEX. I rather hope he quite liked us.
>
> MEG. Yes, I think he did quite like us.
>
> ALEX. I'm not so sure.

MEG. Why?

> *Pause.*

What? Did I witter?

ALEX. Mm?

MEG. I said, 'did I witter?'

ALEX. I wouldn't call it wittering.

MEG. Oh. What would you call it?

ALEX. I don't know. More of a sort of vast oral
incontinence.

MEG. Do you want cocoa?

ALEX. God. Look, Meg, do you think he minded when I
said he could pick up his chicken bone?

MEG. Yes, I do. You embarrassed him. Besides, I'd
already picked mine up. The obvious thing to do with
these people is to show them by example. Anyway,
he was doing very well with his knife and fork.

ALEX. No, he wasn't. That's why I suggested he should
pick it up in the first place.

MEG. Well, I was doing very well with my knife and
fork. And he was doing very well with his knife and
fork.

ALEX. I don't think you ought to talk to him about his
headaches though.

MEG. Why?

ALEX. It embarrassed him.

MEG. It did not embarrass him. You embarrassed him a
lot more talking about his parents, trying to force a
lift on him down to Scunthorpe.

ALEX. Well. It's better than giving him diarrhoea by
forcing fig rolls down his throat, my God.

MEG. Look, Alex. I've tried very hard with Trevor and the
least you can do is show me some gratitude. It's
utterly selfish of you.

So the scene that ended up in the play was totally different from the scene suggested in the scenario, but one that had been arrived at equally organically and which better served the same dramatic purpose.

I work my way through the scenario, structuring each scene as I go and end up with a rough version of the final play.

The Final Script

The next part of the process is to hone and polish each of the scenes and to rehearse them in detail as one would a conventional script. Even at this stage it is important to allow exploration of the unexpected.

In Act One, Scene Five, Julie arrives at the bar and finds Wayne and Philip getting drunk. After a brief period of insulting Julie while impersonating Popeye and Bluto, Philip goes to the bar and returns with drinks and crisps. Philip and Julie then discuss house-hunting while Wayne plays with his crisp packet. In one improvisation Wayne managed to explode the bag, showering crisps all over the immaculate Julie. Philip and Wayne thought this was incredible funny and went into a routine about Irish crisps and the Lone Ranger, ignoring Julie who stormed off. Philip had to persuade her to come back. The crisp incident raised the stakes in the scene and so became part of the final version. Philip had to work harder to keep Julie on side. Julie now had leverage to make Philip go house-hunting, and the Wayne/Julie relationship took on a new dimension throughout the rest of the play.

I usually arrive at a final script in time for the last couple of run-throughs before the dress rehearsal. Only then is anything written down; and this is primarily to provide technical, sound and lighting cues.

The music and songs for *A Bed of Roses* were written by the whole company after the improvisation period and as the play was being scripted. The idea was that the style of the song in someway reflected the character who performed it, thus Trevor's song became a Johnny Cash country-and-western number, and Philip's song was a punk anthem constructed out of TV theme tunes.

The process is slightly different when making a play with a shorter rehearsal period. The character work, life history and background research are exactly the same, but the exploratory improvisation period is much shorter. Often this results in working towards a master improvisation, the one event that the play focuses on.

The BBC television play *Games Without Frontiers* was set in the bar/disco on the midnight ferry from Holland to Harwich. Philip Jackson and Jim Broadbent were two married men from Retford who had been on a dirty weekend to Amsterdam. Christopher Fairbank was a soldier from Liverpool on leave with a broken ankle. Helen Cooper was a Dutch art student on her way to an experimental therapy course in London. I worked with the actors in England creating the characters and setting up their potential relationships then took them to Amsterdam for a couple of days. Here we both discussed and set up improvisations on location that determined the events that took place in Holland before the return ferry trip. Phil and Jim went to a live sex show in character. Fairbank fell into a canal.

Back in the BBC Pebble Mill rehearsal room we recreated the bar and disco area of the boat and set up an improvisation in real time, during which the characters met each other and the story of the midnight boat trip was played out. This was the master improvisation. The job then was to map out the essence of what had happened in this improvisation and to distil the five-hour boat journey into a fifty-minute script. Equipped with the resulting scenario we began to structure the material. At the same time as working on the script with the central characters, I worked with another group of actors on creating the other passengers on the ferry. I then set up a series of shorter improvisations that explored the events on *their* journey. I now had two parallel narratives: the story of the central characters and the story of the other passengers. The next stage was to interweave the two, thus Jim Broadbent's character encountered an incompetent Buddhist pretending to meditate on the way to the lavatory, and there was a subplot in which the barman tried to hire out his cabin for dodgy sexual liaisons. All the scenes in the final piece had been created in response to the master improvisation, but several of them had been created separately from it.

All of which goes to show that the method varies every time, and can and should be modified to accommodate the various eccentricities of whatever situation one finds oneself working in.

So to briefly sum up:

The Twelve-Step Plan

1) The actors prepare a list of people they know who they are interested in playing.
2) The director works individually with each actor discussing characters. After several days of storytelling, the director decides which character the actor will pursue.
3) The director and the actor construct a detailed life history of the character – usually a combination of fact (i.e. information the actor has about his chosen subject) and fiction (i.e. that which the actor and director invent).
4) Research. The actor investigates the world of the character (i.e. information on education, profession, religion, etc.).

5) Visualisation exercises. The actor begins to think him or herself into character.
6) Creating an environment. The actor creates the character's room and inhabits it. The actor experiments with the character's physicality and voice.
7) Going for a walk. The actor takes the character for a walk, goes shopping, feeds the ducks, sees the world through the character's eyes.
8) The director begins to create relationships between the characters and sets up the conditions and circumstances for the narrative to unfold.
9) The main improvisation period. The director orchestrates the chronological improvisations from which the story of the play will emerge.
10) The director writes a scenario suggested by the events explored in the main improvisation period.
11) The director and the actors structure the play and finalise the dialogue.
12) The play is rehearsed in the same way as any other.

The Rules of the Game

- Everything that happens in the rehearsal room must remain a secret until the play is written. 'Loose lips sink ships.'
- Actors must never discuss their characters with other actors.
- In discussion, actors must always refer to their characters in the third person.
- Actors must always 'warm up' into character before any improvisation.

- In improvisations, actors must not invent spurious information for dramatic or comic effect.
- Actors must remain in character until the director says 'cut'.

As I said at the beginning, this chapter is merely a rough guide to the way I work. The process I have described generates characters and material that can be used to tell a story. It's up to the individual director to decide what to do with it. The process of deciding which material to include and which to reject is more usually described as *writing a play*…

A BED OF ROSES
by Mike Bradwell

A *Bed of Roses* was first performed at the Traverse Theatre, Edinburgh, by the Hull Truck Theatre Company as part of the Edinburgh Festival Fringe in August 1977. The cast was as follows:

REV. ALEX BRIDIE	Robin Soans
MEG BRIDIE	Kathy Iddon
TREVOR DUCKER	Alan Williams
PHILIP de BURGER	David Threlfall
JULIE CARSON	Heather Tobias
MEL	Mia Soteriou
WAYNE	Colin Goddard
Director	Mike Bradwell
Designer	Gemma Jackson

Characters

REV. ALEX BRIDIE
MEG BRIDIE
TREVOR DUCKER
PHILIP de BURGER
JULIE CARSON
MEL
WAYNE

ACT ONE

Scene One

The church.

Playover music: 'All People that On Earth Do Dwell'. ALEX
enters pulpit.

ALEX. Good morning, it's nice to see you all here. Next Sunday
is the nineteenth after Trinity – Holy Communion will be at
8.30, the – family service as usual at eleven o'clock, and
evensong next Sunday is at 6.30. Thursday is St Simon and
St Jude the Apostle's day, so that's a celebration of Holy
Communion here at 8.30, and it would make quite a
change if I wasn't the only person here. The pram service
this week is three o'clock on Wednesday in the Meeting
Hall. Oh, and there's something else – ah, yes – my wife has
asked me to remind you that – we're about to embark on
the CMS knitting month. I'm sure she'll be happy to supply
you – with further details and the right-sized needles in the
name of the Father, the Son and the Holy Ghost. Amen.

Who is your house open to? Who is your house open to?
When I first came to this city, I was walking through the
Market Square and I decided to go into Holy Trinity to pray
– but the door was locked. So I went to St Mary's, Lowgate –
and that was locked as well. So I tried St Alban's, St Michael
and All Angels, St Bartholomew's, St Botolph's – they were
all locked. All of them. And when I got to this church I
couldn't even get at the doors because the gates at the
bottom of the path were chained and padlocked. So I made
a few enquiries and I always got the same answer: 'We can't
afford a verger.' 'I see – what do you need a verger for?'
'Isn't it obvious?' they would reply. 'It's to keep out the
thieves, the tramps, the drunks and the hooligans.' So who
is your house open to? As Christians, I mean. As Christians
would you really welcome strangers in here – or tramps –
niggers, Krauts, wops, Eyeties, Jews? I mean, Jews? – Where
the whole thing began? In the second lesson today we heard
the parable of the hundred sheep. Now, God trusted the
ninety and nine – he went after the hundredth sheep, the
stray sheep, the tramp, the drunk and the hooligan. So it

34

seems, does it not, that most of our churches specifically bar their doors to keep out the very people who God is most anxious should come in. Actually, did you ever hear anything so bloody stupid? As members of the church, you – we – are missionaries. Rather than preoccupying ourselves with the amount of carpeting on the vestry floor we should be spreading the Christian ideals to all of those living within the compass of this parish – all of them. God help us, there are people dying of hypothermia in this parish. There are people living lonely and despairing lives and they're just waiting – waiting for a hand to help them out of the rut. And that must be a friendly hand, and it must be a Christian hand, and it must be your hand. They're knocking at your door. There was one other church I visited on that first morning. Outside there was a large notice and it said 'Christ will come again soon. Are you – underlined – ready to receive him?' And you know that was the ultimate hypocrisy because the doors of that church were bolted and barred. Who is your house open to?

And may the words of my mouth and the thoughts of all our hearts be now and always acceptable in Thy sight, O Lord, my strength and my redeemer. Amen.

Fade. The COMPANY *enter to sing a happy-clappy contemporary hymn.*

ALL.
Hand in hand,
Hand in hand,
From land to land,
Brothers and sisters,
Hand in hand.

Love shall come unto,
Love shall come unto,
Love shall come unto me,
As the waters cover the,
Waters cover the sea.

Hand in hand,
Hand in hand,
From land to land,
Brothers and sisters,
Hand in hand.

35

Scene Two

The visiting room in the prison.

MEG *and* TREVOR *sit at the table on which is a packet of fig rolls, two cans of cherryade and ten Player's No. 10 cigarettes.*

MEG (*reading from parish magazine*). 'My third is in roar which you hear but don't see, my fourth is in what this is meant to be, my fifth is a circle and somewhere in coke, and my sixth you will find in felt but not folk'... Do you like it? Well, you can have it if you like, it's okay. I've got plenty of copies. Oh, and if you feel like working it out, there's the clue at the bottom of the page. Have another fig roll. It's lovely to see you eating and drinking again, Trevor. What was it you had last time? Tummy upset? Anyway, you feel okay now, don't you? It's so exciting, isn't it? Only ten days! I bet you can't wait to get out to a pub; have a pint. We're really looking forward to you coming to dinner that night, Trevor. Oh, that reminds me. I meant to tell you. I'm in the middle of organising a Christmas party. It's going to be for the Womens' and Mens' Fellowship combined. It's going to be a sort of fancy-dress-ball affair – you know the sort of thing. Anyway, I was actually looking for someone to help me do the decorations and I wondered if perhaps you might be interested.

TREVOR. Yeah.

MEG. Oh, good, super. Thank you. Oh, and I'm so pleased you're joining the film society because on the first Saturday you get out – we're showing *The Loneliness of the Long Distance Runner*. Have you seen it? No? Well, you'll love it, you really will. Oh yes, and another thing I was going to mention, was the football. I mean, I know you're not interested in sports or anything like that but you see we do have this sort of church football side as it were and anyway the whole thing about it is that you don't have to be any good to be on it because my husband, for example, he plays on the, er... on the west wing and he's absolutely hopeless so I mean to say if you were to join – feel very...

TREVOR. But I can't play football.

MEG. No, I know, but what I'm trying to say is that you don't even have to be any good. I meant to say you don't even have to know the rules.

TREVOR. No, I can't play. I had an accident, you see, I did me head and and me lungs in.

MEG. I'm sorry, Trevor. I didn't know about that. When was that?

TREVOR. It was when I was about four. I got run over.

MEG. Was it very serious?

TREVOR. Yeah. I was in hospital about four years on and off.

MEG. What did you have? Concussion?

TREVOR. I cracked me fucking skull open.

MEG. Oh well, in that case naturally I won't mention the football again, Trevor. Unless of course you want to come along and support the side. I mean to say you could always come along and cheer the side on, couldn't you, if you felt like it?

Pause.

She offers a fig roll. He refuses.

Cigarette? (*Lights his cigarette.*) Anyway, you got my letter, didn't you? What about your parents. Have they written to you at all? No? What about your brother? How long's he got left?

TREVOR. Well, he's got a few years, hasn't he.

MEG. Yes, I suppose he has. Well, I expect you'll pop down and see them when you get out, won't you, I mean…

VOICE. Time.

MEG. I mean, you'll pop down and see your parents, won't you? Well, Trevor, it's pram service for me this afternoon, two for the price of one. That's what they call us, you know – vicars' wives, I mean. You know, wife and secretary as well and general organiser of everything else really. Have a final fig roll. It's going to be a real field day for my husband; these are his favourite biscuits. Well, Trevor, we'll see you on Monday week then, about seven o'clock. And you're quite happy about getting around to the house on your own? I mean, you don't want a lift or anything? – No? Well, we'll see you, bye-bye, Trevor. (*Shakes his hand.*)

TREVOR. Thanks for coming.

MEG. Oh, it's a pleasure. Bye-bye.

TREVOR. Bye.

She goes.

Scene Three

The bar.

PHILIP *and* WAYNE *sit at small table on bar stools with pint glasses. Muzak in background.* PHILIP *tears up cigarette packet. They laugh.*

PHILIP. We had this bloke phone up today. You know we've got this 'Spot-the-Car' competition in the paper; picture of a car, registration number, if it's your car you come into the office and get twenty pounds' worth of vouchers to spend at the garage. This bloke phones up today and he said ''Ello!' and I said 'Hello!' and he said ''Ello!' and I said 'HELLO!' And he said 'I've been a reader of your paper for fifty years.' So I said 'Oh yes, you must be tired.' So he said ''ELLO!' and I said 'HELLO!' So he said 'No – it's about this 'ere "Spot-the-Car" competition, you see.' So I said 'Oh Christ, Bob, we've got a winner.' You see. So he said he'd been 'looking'.

WAYNE. 'Having a look.'

PHILIP. 'Looking at this picture,' he said 'for about arf an hour and I'm pretty sure it's an Austin Allegro.'

WAYNE (*as John Cleese*). Too silly, too silly.

PHILIP. Boring.

WAYNE. Spot-the-looney.

PHILIP. Spot- the-looney.

WAYNE. Eh, it's 'take the bra off the deb' and 'spot-the-Bristols'.

PHILIP. I know who'd win that.

WAYNE. Who?

PHILIP. Fay.

WAYNE. 'Where's Fay.'

PHILIP. 'Where's Fay.' God, Fay – *big*!

WAYNE Beautiful. (*Imitates car hooter.*)

PHILIP. Do you remember that night.

WAYNE. Eh! 'Luigi – we-no-take-a-de-Barclay-Card.'

PHILIP. 'Bianco!' I came back from the bathroom and she was spark out on the bed. Spark out.

WAYNE. In a coma.

PHILIP. Comatose interruptus, mate. So it's off with the kecks.

WAYNE. 'Naughty, naughty.'

PHILIP. 'Smack my botty.'

WAYNE. 'Smack my botty.' (*As Eddie Waring*.) 'Up and under, Frank.'

PHILIP. 'Up and under, round the blind side.' Oh, Fay. Eh, come on, Wayne – you do pick them, don't you!

WAYNE. Who?

PHILIP. You, weasel-face. Marjorie!

WAYNE. Marjorie. Sick. Don't talk to me about sick. She was sick up the stairs, she was sick in the salon – she was even sick in me aquarium. (*Scots accent*.) 'Eh, Jimmy – d'ye know what I do wi' bills I don't agree wi'?'

PHILIP. What.

WAYNE. Aquarium.

PHILIP (*simultaneous*). Ralph.

WAYNE (*simultaneous*). Hughie.

They pretend to throw up. Pause.

How is Julie then?

PHILIP. Oh, she's thick. Eh, listen, she went into the building society yesterday, to put some of my money in, and she said to the bloke behind the counter – (*Irish accent*.) 'Eh, you!!'

WAYNE (*Irish Belfast accent*). 'Eh, you!'

PHILIP. 'Eh, you, Eamon, you I want to put some of me and my fiancé's money in here, right.' So he said 'Certainly, madam, have you got any indentifi – you know, can you identify yourself?' So she puts her hand in her handbag, pulls out a mirror and says, 'Oh yes, I tink that's me all right!'

WAYNE. You mean she's so thick she thought Sheffield Wednesday was a public holiday.

PHILIP. She was the one who thought Muffin the Mule was a sexual offence.

WAYNE. She thought Sherlock Holmes was a block of flats.

PHILIP. She went into the baker's and threatened to sue him for forging her signature on the hot-cross buns.

Laughter. PHILIP *resumes tearing a cigarette packet.*

WAYNE. Eh, what are you doing – making confetti? You know, big day.

PHILIP. Big off, Biggles. Eh – you got a light. (*Pokes his nose through two fingers of the 'V' sign.*)

WAYNE. Eh, you've not had a cig all day, have you.

PHILIP. Aaah. (*Chinese accent.*) 'Glasshopper, you reary velly quick.' No, I had this dream.

WAYNE. Yeah?

PHILIP. Yeah. There was me and Julie in this dream and we were going through this cornfield – lovely sunny day – and we were married and we had two kids with us – you know, one of each, and they were skipping through this cornfield and tugging at me and shouting 'Daddy, Daddy.' And I turned round and I dropped dead of cancer.

WAYNE. Do you want another drink?

Blackout. Muzak increases in volume, changes to Vivaldi.

Scene Four

The vicarage.

MEG, ALEX *and* TREVOR *cluster round the door.*

MEG. Well, it's been lovely, Trevor, so glad you were able to come and perhaps you'll come again some time.

ALEX. Look, Trevor, I'm absolutely serious, any time you want anything, now that's food or money or clothes, please, please feel free to come round here. It's an ever open door, right?

MEG. Well, at least telephone first, Trevor, cos there's not always someone at home.

ALEX. Look, Trevor, for God's sake, don't go and nick anything or if you do come and nick it off us cos we don't mind...

MEG. Trevor, would you like a lift home because it's no problem at all, the car is just outside the door.

ALEX. And if you've nowhere better to go for Christmas come and have Christmas here, you can even stay if you like.

MEG. Yes, well, darling, we'll see him at the film on Saturday, won't we, so bye-bye then, Trevor.

ALEX. Yes, yes.

TREVOR. Thanks for the tea.

MEG. Oh, it was a pleasure, bye-bye.

ALEX. Not at all, not at all, nice to see you, look, Trevor, come and see us again soon, all right?

MEG. Bye.

TREVOR. Ta-ra. (*Goes.*)

ALEX. Can you find your way all right? Night-night.

> MEG *sits.* ALEX *practises cricket strokes with a backscratcher.*

MEG. Well, fancy him knowing anything about Martin Luther King. Do you suppose he read about him in a book?

ALEX. No, darling, I expect they met at a garden party on the White House lawn.

MEG. Well, fancy him not telling me he was a Roman Catholic. What do Martin Luther King and Roman Catholicism have in common?

ALEX. They both died in the sixties.

MEG. No, I'm serious. I can't fathom him out. Fancy him bringing that Newcastle Brown Ale. Awfully sweet. Did you like him?

ALEX. Yes, very much.

MEG. What do you mean, 'very much'?

ALEX. Very much.

MEG. Well, you can't like him very much, you don't know him very well.

ALEX. You don't keep your mouth shut very often, but it's very pleasant when you do.

MEG. I wonder what he thought of us?

ALEX. I rather hope he quite liked us.

MEG. Yes, I think he did quite like us.

ALEX. I'm not so sure.

MEG. Why?

ALEX. Oh God, I don't know, it's just that I sometimes wonder whether it all gets in the way.

MEG. What?

ALEX. Uppingham, the public-school voice, this bloody collar.

MEG. What's that got to do with it? (*Pause.*) Mm? (*Pause.*) Have I upset you? (*Pause.*) Did I witter?

ALEX. Mm?

MEG. I said 'did I witter?'

ALEX. No, I wouldn't call it wittering.

MEG. Oh. What would you call it?

ALEX. I don't know. More of a sort of vast oral incontinence.

MEG. Do you want some cocoa?

ALEX. God. (*Pause.*) Look, Meg, do you think he minded when I said he could pick up his chicken bone?

MEG. Yes, I do. You embarrassed him. Besides, I'd already picked mine up. The obvious thing to do with these people is to show them by example. Anyway, he was doing very well with his knife and fork.

ALEX. No, he wasn't. That's why I suggested he should pick it up in the first place.

MEG. Well, I was doing very well with my knife and fork, because the meat was falling off the bone. And he was doing very well with his knife and fork.

ALEX. Sure as a boar?

MEG. I'm certain as a curtain. I thought he was absolutely marvellous about everything. I mean to say he's awfully sweet, isn't he? I mean, he's utterly inoffensive.

ALEX. Yes. I don't think you ought to talk to him about his headaches though.

MEG. Why not?

ALEX. It embarrassed him.

MEG. It did not embarrass him. He told me about his headaches ages ago of his own free will. You embarrassed him a lot more talking about his parents, trying to force a lift on him down to Scunthorpe.

ALEX. Well, it's better than giving him diarrhoea by forcing fig rolls down his throat, my God.

MEG. Look, Alex. I've tried very hard with Trevor and the least you can do is talk to me about him, utterly selfish of you. You show no gratitude whatsoever.

ALEX. Gratitude for what?

MEG. Gratitude for me giving up my free time encouraging him to come round here. No gratitude, no encouragement, nothing.

Pause.

ALEX. It's a mess, isn't it?

Fade. Vivaldi music which changes into muzak background to next scene.

Scene Five

The bar.

Same as before except more beer has been drunk. PHILIP *is coughing.*

WAYNE. 'What's the matter, Malcolm?'

PHILIP. 'Oh, Mum, I can't take my exams blocked up like this, can I?'

WAYNE. 'Course you can, Malcolm!'

Enter JULIE. *Bit of business before* WAYNE *points out that* JULIE *has arrived.*

PHILIP (*as Bruce Forsyth*). 'All right, my love, over here, over here.' Hello, Finickey.

JULIE. Hello, Chelmsford.

WAYNE. Hello, Julie.

JULIE. Hiya, Wayne.

PHILIP. 'All right, dear – good good. Give us a twirl then, Anthea. Come on, give Wayne a twirl – let's all see it. Right, we've all seen it now, sit down. Kissy, kissy – Oh! Nice, Bruce's room later if you're lucky. What've you got here?'

JULIE. Housing lists.

PHILIP. Oooh, housing lists, Wayne. 'Right, come here! All right, Wayne – first question's for a pound. "What's the

43

difference between Stork SB and a bucket of shit?" – Answer – "The bucket."

They laugh.

There you go – Julie, is it? – Let's have a look at the old scoreboard. Very nice to insult you. Didn't she do well, Wayne!'

WAYNE. Triffic.

PHILIP. Oh, triffic, yeah. 'Where do you come from, dear? Tell us where you come from.'

JULIE. Philip! Please.

PHILIP. Tell Wayne where you come from.

JULIE. Belfast.

WAYNE (*as John Cleese*). 'Don't mention the war.'

PHILIP. 'Que Signor Fawlty?'

WAYNE. 'Don't mention the war.'

JULIE. Philip, there are people around.

PHILIP. 'Yes, very good, there are people around – yer, in fact the place would be deserted really, apart from these people.' And Wayne. 'John Wayne – this is Julie Andrews. Julie Andrews – this is John Wayne.'

WAYNE. 'That's a Wayne with a "Y" not an "I".'

PHILIP (*simultaneous*). Boom, boom!

WAYNE (*simultaneous*). Boom, boom!

JULIE. Philip, I haven't got a drink.

PHILIP (*moves his glass in front of her*). 'There you go, sunshine. Wait a moment, though. (*As Eric Morecombe.*) 'Little Ern, who's this I see coming down the road? It's Spotty Dog.'

JULIE. How long have you been here, Philip?

PHILIP (*as Kermit*). 'Will you get out of here, Miss Piggy?'

JULIE. Are you drunk?

WAYNE (*Popeye laugh*). Aaag-gag-gag-gag.

PHILIP *joins in.*

PHILIP. 'Okay, Bluto.'

WAYNE. 'Okay, Popeye – dis is it.'

PHILIP. 'Aag-gag-gag-gag.'

WAYNE. 'Aag-gag-gag-gag'

JULIE. Popeye didn't do that.

PHILIP. What?

JULIE. Well, I never saw Popeye do that. (*Pause.*) Well, I didn't, but.

PHILIP (*as Flowerpot Men*). 'Weed.'

JULIE. Well, who's that supposed to be?

PHILIP. I don't know. Mrs Popeye?

JULIE. Popeye wasn't married.

PHILIP *leaves to get her a drink, makes sign of the vampire behind her back.*

WAYNE. Oh, he's really funny, Phil, isn't he; really a scream.

JULIE. D'you think so.

Pause.

WAYNE. Have you had your hair cut?

JULIE. No.

WAYNE. Oh, it suits you like that. I mean, most people come in the salon, they want all these modern styles, but yours looks good like that. You know, it suits your bones – hangs really well. You ought to get your hair hennaed, you know.

JULIE. I don't want to get my hair dyed.

WAYNE. Oh, it's not dyed – it brings out the natural –

PHILIP (*as John Noakes*). 'All right, break it up – because we've had a really *Blue Peter* beezin' bazzin' time at the bar. We've got some *Blue Peter* crisps for Wayne, and a drink for Val, who's on a *Blue Peter* special assignment. Hello, Val!'

JULIE. Philip, I had these lists through this morning from Cundall Wells.

PHILIP. Ooh, not Cundall Lingus I hope.

JULIE. Philip, you're terrible.

PHILIP. Ooh, come on. (*Kisses her.*)

JULIE. Philip, look, there's one here.

PHILIP. Where?

JULIE. St David's Close.

PHILIP. Is he?

> *At this point* WAYNE *spills contents of crisp packet over* JULIE.

JULIE. Do you mind, Wayne!

WAYNE. I'm sorry, they usually come out of the top.

PHILIP. They must be Irish crisps! Come here, Wayne, I'm starving.

JULIE. Philip, have you not had your tea yet?

PHILIP. 'And next week, Wayne, we'll show you in the *Blue Peter* studio how to make an Hawaiian guitar out of a wooden chair and three elastic *Blue Peter* bands!

> WAYNE *makes car-hooter noise.*

Fuck off, Petra!'

WAYNE. 'Get down, Patch!'

JULIE. Philip, you promised me we were going to look at houses tonight, so you did.

PHILIP. I didn't. White woman speako with forko tongue-o. Ooh! Wayne! 'Kimosabe. Coach come past here, Kimosabe. Four wooden wheels. Three horses on front. One black one one white one and one with a bit of... on foot. Four parcels of luggage on top. Three men inside and only one woman.' (*Changes voices.*) 'That's amazing, Tonto, how do you know that?' (*Change back to first voice.*) 'Fucking coach run over me, Kimosabe!'

> *They laugh.*

Boom, boom!

> PHILIP *pokes* JULIE *with his elbow.*

JULIE. Philip, don't do that; that hurts.

PHILIP (*as Edna Everage*). 'Sorry, Joan dear, just poking around. Pokey, pokey, pokey.'

JULIE. Are you coming or not!

PHILIP. Pardon. (*As Frank Spencer.*) 'What are you giggling at, Wayne? Nah, don't giggle, cos we've been having a bit of harassment with our sex life, haven't we, Betty. So I went to the doctor's, you see, and I said "Hello, doctor," and he said

"Hello." So he said "You've got to jump on her and make love to her when she least expects it." So I thought – ooh, nice. So we were having tea the other night and I said "Pass us the jam," and I thought – right, now on the table and…'

JULIE *leaves.*

Did you say something? Hang on, wrong time of the month. (*Walks over to* JULIE.) What's wrong?

JULIE. You promised me we'd look at houses tonight.

PHILIP. I didn't.

JULIE. You did.

PHILIP. I didn't. I didn't know he was going to be here tonight.

JULIE. I thought we were going to be together tonight, Philip.

PHILIP. We are.

JULIE. Huh! (*Looks across at* WAYNE.)

PHILIP. Look, Julie, I can't leave him now, he'll be on his own.

JULIE. So. Oh, Philip, come on, let's go.

    Pause.

PHILIP. One more drink.

JULIE. No, I can't go back over there.

PHILIP. Why not?

JULIE. I look silly, that's why. Oh, come on, Philip.

PHILIP. Look, we can look at houses any night, right?

JULIE. I don't just want to look at houses, you know, Philip.

PHILIP. What do you want to do then?

JULIE. Philip. Come on. (*Kisses him.*)

    They embrace.

PHILIP. Oh, all right. You do realise I'll have to limp across there now.

JULIE. Shhh!

    They cross to WAYNE.

PHILIP (*as Frank Spencer*). ''Ere, Wayne. Mind you we can't eat at Wimpey's any more, cos we've been banned.'

JULIE. We're going, Wayne, cheerio.

47

PHILIP. What she means, Wayne, is that she's going – probably – and I'm probably going with her.

WAYNE. Okay. I'll see you then.

PHILIP. Yeah, see you.

WAYNE. I'll give you a ring.

> As PHILIP *exits, he points out the engagement ring on* JULIE's *finger. Fade.*

Scene Six

TREVOR's *bedsit.*

Sound of electronic white noise. MEL *and* TREVOR *sit at a table.* TREVOR *fiddles with a broken radio, source of the noise.*

MEL. It doesn't work.

TREVOR. What?

MEL. I said it doesn't work.

TREVOR. You gonna flog it then?

MEL. Yeah, I'm gonna flog it, but I'm not gonna flog it like that – we got to get it working first.

TREVOR. Tell them the batteries are flat.

MEL. Oh, come on, Trev. You think they're stupid? They're gonna try it out – we got to fix it. So what's the matter with it?

TREVOR. It doesn't work.

MEL. Trevor, I know it doesn't work... You know what I think it is? It's cos it doesn't have an aerial – we get an aerial, it'll be all right... (*Takes a cigarette.*)

TREVOR. What you doing?

MEL. What do you mean – I'm having a fag –

TREVOR. Well, they're fucking mine, them, you cunt.

MEL. Trevor, all right, I know they're yours – look, I get some money tomorrow, I buy some. You get it back, okay?

TREVOR. You'll get some money this afternoon when you've flogged this.

MEL. So how much did it cost you?

TREVOR. I don't know.

MEL. What do you mean, you don't know? How much did you pay for it –

TREVOR. I don't know.

MEL. Trevor, you must've paid something for it.

TREVOR. I don't fucking know. Our kid gave it to us.

MEL. What, he gave you that? I didn't know.

TREVOR. Yeah. He gave us a few.

MEL *laughs.*

What you laughing at, you cunt?

MEL. What?

TREVOR. Come on, what are you fucking laughing at? What's so funny?

MEL. What? Trevor, what?

TREVOR. What, what, what –

MEL. Trevor, come on, you can laugh about anything, right?

TREVOR. Oh, that's fucking clever, isn't it. That's fucking real. You can't laugh at anything. You can't laugh at something like murder, can you?

MEL. Yeah. Course you can laugh about anything – about murder. Yeah… Trevor, we go through this every day, you know?

TREVOR. Yeah – I'll tell you one thing you can't laugh about.

MEL. Yeah? What.

TREVOR. You can't laugh about rape, can you?

MEL. Maybe, yeah… All right, Trevor, look. I couldn't laugh while it was happening to me, but I could afterwards. Yeah. I can laugh at rape, okay?

TREVOR. Fucking good job, that.

MEL. Yeah? Why.

TREVOR. Course only Frank knows you're here, and he's fucking mental, isn't he? You know? – If anything happened to you.

MEL. What are you talking – about?

TREVOR. And Frank's mental anyway, so they wouldn't believe him –

MEL. Come on, what are you talking about. *Ma che cazzata dici? Tu, sei pazzo* –

TREVOR. Talk fucking sense to me, right?

MEL. All right, Trevor… all right… Boy, I dunno, ya know, Trevor, I've met some jerks in my time – cos that's what you are. You're a jerk, right?

TREVOR. Say that again.

MEL. You're a jerk.

> TREVOR *throws an ashtray at her. Blackout. Loud electronic music leading into Chinese linking music.*

Scene Seven

WAYNE *and* PHILIP *with telephones are lit in individual spots either side of the stage. The phone rings.*

WAYNE. 'Herro?'

PHILIP Oh, 'Herro.'

WAYNE. 'Ah, One-Long-Bang Chop Suey House?'

PHILIP. 'Ah, good heaving, heavy body. How are you?'

WAYNE. Fine. Listen, do you want to come to the Bitter End Ball tonight?

PHILIP. What's that?

WAYNE. You know, dancing, bar, disco, puppet show, that sort of thing.

PHILIP. No, thanks.

WAYNE. Hot Chocolate are playing.

PHILIP. Oh, great, I'll shave all my hair off then.

WAYNE. You can bring Julie if you want.

> PHILIP *laughs.*

All right, it's only a joke!

PHILIP. No, it's off.

WAYNE. Listen, squire, plenty of spare there. I'm taking Pam, our new stylist.

PHILIP. Do you want to buy a ring then?

WAYNE. Say no more. Look, why don't you come with us, have a few jars. We can go in Pam's car.

PHILIP. No, I'm staying in and watching *Planet of the Apes*.

WAYNE. Yeah, all right, suit yourself. No one else will.

PHILIP. Yeah.

WAYNE. I'll give you a ring. Cheers then.

PHILIP. Cheers.

Fade.

Scene Eight

TREVOR's *bedsit.*

Electronic music. TREVOR *and* MEL *sit at table. There is a Bible.* MEL *holds a dice in a spoon over a candle flame. They are playing a black magic fortune-telling game.*

MEL. Belial… Belial… Belial… come in, Belial, do you read me?

TREVOR. Shut up –

MEL. What? Look, do you want me to do this thing or not?

TREVOR. Do it.

MEL. Okay… Belial… Belial… Belial… Oh, come on, Trev, I feel stupid sitting here going 'Belial, Belial' –

TREVOR. Concentrate!

MEL. All right, I'm concentrating. Belial… Belial… Belial… Belial…

TREVOR. All right – is it hot yet?

MEL *holds the dice in her hand – burns herself.*

MEL (*reading dice*). Two. (*Looks up fortunes list.*) 'Marry a millionaire.' Well, that's a fucking stupid answer. How am I gonna marry a millionaire?

51

TREVOR. Course it's stupid – (*Moves to bed.*)

MEL. Yeah, that's what I thought before we started.

TREVOR. Cos ya were mucking about with it.

MEL. What do you mean, I was mucking about with it?

TREVOR. Shut up. You can't fool me.

MEL. I feel sick.

TREVOR. So?

MEL. Fucking freezing in here, do you know that? Oh boy, I like that, Trevor, I really like that; you get me up at four in the morning to do this crap.

TREVOR. You can't muck about with it.

MEL. All right, we won't muck about with it. Belial's obviously a dead loss. Won't try him again. Who else have we got? Phregaton. Maybe he's in. Okay, here we go. Phregaton… Phregaton…

TREVOR (*knocking candle over*). What are you doing?! Stop it, you cunt!

MEL. What's the matter with you?

TREVOR. Stop it, it's fucking dangerous, that.

MEL. Trevor, it's all a load of wank.

TREVOR. It's dangerous.

MEL. All right, Trev, tell me something. Is it to do with this Bible stuff? Eh? Come on. What's all this shit you've written in here? I didn't know you had a thing about religion. Trevor, listen, it's all a load of crap. It's all up here.

TREVOR. No, it's not, you know it's all up here.

MEL. This got something to do with that metal plate you got in your head, Trev, eh?

TREVOR. See, you know nowt, you.

MEL. No, no, but at least I don't wake up in the middle of the night with the screaming abdabs do I, like some people –

TREVOR. All right, I'll tell you. I know a bloke got killed through messing about with all this.

MEL. What, with these Astragoth guys?

TREVOR. Yeah, like you.

MEL. All right, Trev, I got a proposition for you. What would happen, right, if I called them all a bunch of slobs – what they gonna do to me?

TREVOR. Shut up!

MEL. Bunch of slobs! Come on, Trevor, what if I chuck the Bible down the lav, what are they gonna do? Nothing, right?

TREVOR. Yeah, well, this bloke got killed.

MEL. So what happened to him?

TREVOR. Well, he died.

MEL. Yeah, how did he die, Trevor?

TREVOR. He got run over.

MEL. Jesus Christ, come on, Trevor, *you* got run over, it's got nothing to do with it – Trev, listen, accidents happen all the time, people get run over every day – I mean, planes crash, people get killed in the war – you think these guys did all that? What's the matter?

TREVOR is staring at something. MEL lifts the table from underneath and makes a ghostly howling noise. TREVOR smashes down the table and gets up.

TREVOR. Oh no. I'm not staying here, you can, I'm going out –

MEL. Hey, Trev, come on, I promise I won't muck about any more, cross my heart and swear on my mother.

TREVOR. I'm going out. (*Exits.*)

MEL (*running to door*). Trevor, come back, you fucking baby! What's the matter with you – *ma, di cosa te paura, non e niente! Eh, vai fan culo* – fucking *cazzo!*

She slams the door. Goes to table. Sets fire to a page of Bible. Crosses herself.

Fade.

TREVOR enters to sing his Johnny Cash song.

TREVOR.
There was a man who took a gun to do the good Lord's will.
He went on down to Texas to find a certain man to kill.
He found his man. He shot him down.
Through the head and through the heart.
And said to him 'I'm sorry, John.
You were a good man from the start.'

53

They took John up to Heaven on a golden ball of fire.
And there he met St Michael and he saw the great Messiah.
And then the Lord Himself came up
With His glory all unfurled.
And He said to John 'These coming days
Will see my fury round the world.'
All the cattle on the prairie will fall down in the rain,
When Joshua and Moses show their faces once again,
And all the living bastards gonna fall right down and cry,
And lift their eyes to Heaven to see the cowboys in the sky.
He's heading out the posse, with Martin on behind.
They're shooting out the evil and the weakness that they
    find.
The Lord has found a good right hand,
Who has no mortal malice.
And that is why they shot John down that awful day in
    Dallas.
Oh, that is why they shot John down that awful day in
    Dallas.

Scene Nine

The vicarage.

ALEX *is sitting,* MEG *in a coat with shopping bags.*

MEG. So anyway, darling, guess what? There was this girl. Sort
    of short dumpy thing with black crinkly hair and scruffy
    jeans on – you know the sort of thing. Anyway, she was
    absolutely sweet, sat me down and gave me a cup of tea,
    and, darling, guess what, she's been living there for a
    month! I mean to say, imagine, Trevor with a girlfriend.
    Although I suppose actually when you come to think of it, if
    he wasn't so spotty he'd be quite good looking. But anyway,
    darling, guess what, he hasn't told her anything about us. I
    mean to say she didn't know who I was. Or you, or anything
    about the Christmas decorations. Anyway, darling, then
    guess what she said to me? She said were we Roman
    Catholics, and then she said were we into supernatural
    religion, because Trevor did things with a Bible and a
    candle and a list with names on it. I mean to say if you ask
    me it sounds as though he's completely and utterly mentally

unhinged. I mean, it sounds like one of those ceremonies, doesn't it? One of those black magic ceremonies. Anyway, darling, then she wouldn't…

ALEX. Meg.

MEG.…tell me any more because apparently…

ALEX. Meg.

MEG.…she doesn't do it, only Trevor…

ALEX *stands*.

ALEX (*loudly*). Meg. Look, sit down a minute, will you? (*Pause.*) I said sit.

MEG *sits*.

Now, no fruit bats, sure as a boar, certain and a curtain.

MEG. Yes.

ALEX. Did you get some more petrol?

MEG. Yes…

ALEX. Now then. Bibles?

MEG. She said to me, 'Trevor reads the Bible.' Well, I never knew Trevor read the Bible. Did you?

ALEX. Reads?

MEG. Well, he does something with it.

ALEX. Candles?

MEG. She said to me did we wank with candles.

ALEX. She said what?

MEG. She said were we into wanking about with candles.

ALEX. Lists?

MEG. Yes, apparently Trevor's got a list with names on it.

ALEX. Names?

MEG. Yes, names.

ALEX. Whose names?

MEG. I don't know. Look, I don't know because she didn't tell me. She doesn't do it apparently. Only Trevor does it.

ALEX. Ceremonies?

MEG. Well, I mean, it must be, mustn't it. I mean, it's black magic.

ALEX. Did I ever tell you about Yeoman Hodges?

MEG. Who?

ALEX. Yeoman Hodges, my old maths master at school?

MEG. Who?

ALEX. He used to invite backward maths students down to his house for extra tuition in the evening. I mean, no one minded going because you got out of the house supper and prep and that sort of thing – and he'd cook you a meal – always the same thing, sausage, mash and beans, and give you a pint of beer. Everyone was convinced he was queer but he never laid a finger on anyone. Anyway, he'd leave you swotting over your extra problems while he went off to get the sausage, mash and beans and the pint of beer. Until one night, a boy called Carrington-Smith got up, crept down the corridor and looked through the keyhole of the kitchen door. And there was Yeoman Hodges, masturbating in the mashed potato.

MEG. That's revolting.

ALEX. Yes – but it does have the added advantage of being true.

Blackout.

JULIE *enters and sings her Irish folk song.*

JULIE.
    My love is like the swans that fly,
    By the shores of Donaghadee.
    My love is like the winds that sigh,
    By the shores of Donaghadee.
    On the waves he rolls over mackerel shoals,
    While the sea bell tolls him back to me,
    By the shores of Donaghadee,
    My love is like the seagull's cry,
    On the shores of Donaghadee.

JULIE *gets into bed.*

Scene Ten

PHILIP *and* JULIE *in bed, under the bedclothes.* PHILIP *hums* Dr Kildare *theme tune. Lights up.*

PHILIP. 'Spanner! Right – that's got the first-aid box open. Get that ironing board out of here. Ooh, it's not an ironing board. Okay, nurse, kiss me.' 'Oh, doctor, no.' 'Kiss me, nurse.' 'Doctor, no!' – 'Nurse, kiss me!' 'Doctor, no – I shouldn't even be in bed with you!'

They laugh.

JULIE. You're terrible, Philip.

PHILIP (*imitating her*). 'I know!' What's going on?

They emerge from under the bedclothes.

(*Sings.*) 'When I take you out for a curry. When I take you out for a curry with the chips on top.' (*Pause.*) 'On our way 'ome. On our way 'ome. Okay, Venus. Okay, Steve. Right, let's go.' (*Does tune from* Fireball XL5.) Eh, did you ever do this when you were a kid. (*Builds up the bedclothes so can play 'cars'. Begins 'driving' a racing car, making a noise.*)

JULIE. Philip, keep the noise down. Mrs McArthy'll hear you.

PHILIP (*German accent*). 'Aah, Mrs McArthy, zo ve meet again. Vell, take zat.' (*Mimes bomb dropping.*)

They laugh

JULIE. Look – there's Wayne!

PHILIP. 'Zo, you are in it too, ja! Zo, take zat und zat und zat.' (*Mimes machine gun.*)

JULIE. Philip, keep the noise down. Mrs McArthy'll hear you. (*Eventually quietens him.*)

PHILIP. Come here. Are you all right, missus?

JULIE. Uh-huh.

PHILIP. If you play your cards right, you can kiss me if you like.

They kiss. They grope around. PHILIP *tries to have sex –* JULIE *is unwilling.*

JULIE. Philip! Stop, it's not safe!

He coughs and dismounts.

I'm sorry I forgot, but I was very upset at the time. Are you angry with me? You are, aren't you? Are you all right? What is it, Philip? You are angry with me. Philip, will you answer me?

While this has been going on, PHILIP *has been wheezing and panting.*

PHILIP. Shut up.

JULIE. What do you mean, 'shut up'?

PHILIP. Stop nagging.

JULIE. I'm not nagging.

PHILIP. You are.

JULIE. I'm not.

PHILIP. You are.

They argue until a climax is reached when JULIE *shouts.*

JULIE. Will you answer me!

PHILIP. What? Are you talking to me?

JULIE. Well, who else do you think I'm talking to?

PHILIP. Who *do* you think you're talking to, Julie? What do you think I am – some kind of wet nurse? I can't take the pill for you, can I? Tell me what it is you want me to do and I'll do it. Tell me, tell me, tell me, come on, tell me tell me – no, don't prompt me, let me guess!

JULIE. I don't want anything.

PHILIP. What? You don't know what you want – you're telling me what I should want. I know what I want but I've always got to please you. I've got to apologise now. Nobody, nobody could please you, Julie, nobody. Not even Brian. No wonder he pissed off and left you. Steve McQueen in *The Great Escape.*

JULIE. You bastard.

PHILIP. If there's so much... You what? Did you say something?!

JULIE. Bastard.

PHILIP. Oooh! 'Bastard.' See, swearing. That's all right for Julie but it's not for Philip. Now, why is that, Julie? Why? Why? (*Begins poking her.*) Why?! Why?! (*Climax of this is that he hits her hard on the arm. Pause.*) I'm sorry.

JULIE. Philip, there are times when I don't know –

PHILIP. What! Well, whose fault is that, then? Oh, of course, it's my fault. It's my fault that when you get me into these states – My fault you make me ill, my fault we've got to be quiet, my fault you forgot to take the pill. You probably did it on purpose anyway to get your own back but it's s-still my fault, isn't it! Why don't you care about what I want for a change? (*Pause.*) I'm glad you asked me cos I'll tell you. Because apart from wanting to get us on *Mr & Mrs* and collect your widow's pension, you're not fucking interested in me.

JULIE. Philip, I love you.

He laughs.

What are you doing? What are you laughing at?

PHILIP. Your face.

There follows an exchange to a climax where JULIE *says...*

JULIE. What are you trying to do to me?!

PHILIP. What am I trying to do to you! Oh, turn 'em off, Julie. (*Has an asthma attack during which he uses inhaler.*)

JULIE. Philip, what is it? Are you all right? Philip, I love you. (*Pause.*) I need you, Philip.

Pause.

PHILIP. It's gone, Julie. Come on, it's gone. I'm okay now, really. Sorry, you know what it's like. Come on. I'm okay. See. Bionic. (*As Columbo.*) 'No, I think you're terrific, Miss Carson. 'Ere, I got a friend to see you. Would you like to see 'im?'

JULIE. Uh-huh.

PHILIP. 'I'll go and get 'im then. Would you wait here, please.' (*Disappears under the bedclothes and returns with an Emu puppet. He plays with it.*)

JULIE. Philip, I want to be a good wife to you.

PHILIP *makes Emu laugh at her.*

Blackout.

During the scene change, we hear the madrigal:

Oh dear God my life is sin,
And I am nought but for they sweet forgiving,
Oh do thou defend me in
My weak and wakeful hours whilst I am living.

Walk I still the tempter's path,
Always the truth denying,
Oh vouchsafe that thou will lift
The burden from my soul as I am dying.

Scene Eleven

TREVOR's *bedsit.*

TREVOR *in bed.* MEL *reading a comic. Knock at the door.* MEL *doesn't answer it. Second knock.* MEL *opens the door.*

MEL. Oh, hello.

ALEX. Hello – Oh, I'm Alex Bridie.

MEL (*virtually closing the door to a crack*). Oh, yeah. I'm Mel.

ALEX. Hello.

MEL. Hello.

ALEX. Is Trevor in?

MEL. Trevor. Yeah, he's in, but he can't see you at the moment –

ALEX. Well, could you tell him it's me?

MEL. Hold on a minute. (*Shuts door on him.*) Hey, Trev, your mate the priest is out there, do you wanna see him?

TREVOR (*asleep*). No...

MEL (*at door*). I'm really sorry, mister, he can't see you, some other time, okay.

Goes to shut the door – ALEX *holds it open.*

ALEX. It is very important.

MEL. Well, maybe I can give him a message or something.

ALEX. No, not really. I wonder what the best way round this is. Could you tell him –

TREVOR. Who is it?

MEL. I guess you'd better come in.

ALEX *enters.*

ALEX. Hello, Trevor, I'm sorry if I've called at an inconvenient time.

TREVOR *starts to get up.*

MEL. I met your wife, you know?

ALEX. Oh yes.

MEL. Yeah. She brought some cakes round.

ALEX. Oh yes, she would.

MEL. Is your church round here then?

ALEX. Yes, it's St Matthew's – that rather hideous brick building up on the main road.

MEL. You do services?

ALEX. Yes, yes, on a Sunday.

MEL. What do you do the rest of the week?

ALEX. Oh, I have about two hundred and seventy meetings and – work about seventy-five hours a day, that sort of thing, you know.

TREVOR. What is it?

ALEX. Ah, yes. Well, it's rather awkward really. I really wanted to have a word with Trevor on his own.

MEL. Oh, yeah, why?

ALEX. Well, actually, it's something you told my wife.

MEL. Oh, I see – Well, if it's something I said, I think I should know about it, don't you?

ALEX. Yes, but it's rather hard for me if you're here.

MEL. Why's it rather hard for you? Look, mister, you can talk in front of me, you know. Look, come on – if it's something I said – Trevor, what do you think?

TREVOR. What is it?

ALEX. Trevor. What you do in your private life is none of my business. But if you start messing around with religion, that is my concern, in my parish at any rate.

TREVOR. What.

ALEX. I've heard that you do things with candles and lists and Bibles and things, and I want to know what it's all about.

MEL *sniggers.*

TREVOR. Shut up, you.

61

ALEX. I've also heard that you indulge in black magic ceremonies, and I want to know if it's true –

MEL. Hey, wait a minute – was that what she told you?

ALEX. Yes.

MEL. Well, it's not true; he doesn't. Trevor, I never said anything like that. I don't know what he's talking about – he's talking rubbish.

TREVOR. What have you been saying, anything?

MEL. No, Trevor, I never said –

TREVOR. What have you been saying?

MEL. Nothing, Trevor –

ALEX. Trevor, listen to me, Trevor – listen. Her exact words were that you wank around with a candle, and a list, and a Bible, and I want to know what it's all about.

MEL. Look, mister, I'll tell you what it's all about. It's a game, you know, names on a bit of paper – it's like consequences – it's just a game –

ALEX. Is it a game, Trevor, or are you playing games with me?

MEL. Look, I've told you – Trevor – tell him it's a game.

ALEX. Trevor, do you indulge in black magic ceremonies, yes or no?

MEL. Look, mister, I don't know what she told you, right, but I do know you've got the wrong end of the stick and you're wasting your time –

ALEX. 'Wrong end of the stick'! 'Wrong end of the stick'! There's bits of burnt Bible in the ashtray – 'wrong end of the stick'? Now, come on, Trevor, tell me, I have a right to know. I am your parish priest. Now tell me, cos I want to know.

TREVOR. Fuck off.

ALEX. No. I'm not leaving this room till I've found out exactly what is going on.

TREVOR (*getting up*). You fucking are –

ALEX. Trevor, sit down and listen. I don't know what the hell you think you're playing at, but I warn you, it's a highly dangerous game, and you need help.

TREVOR. Look, I told you to fucking go.

ALEX. No, I'm not going, I am not going.

TREVOR. You fucking are.

TREVOR pounces on ALEX. MEL breaks up the scuffle, and ALEX flees. MEL slams the door shut. TREVOR smashes furniture.

The fucking bastard! What did you fucking tell him, cos you're gonna fucking get it for that. What did you fucking tell him!

MEL. I didn't tell him anything. Trevor, come on, I didn't tell them anything – Trevor, they don't... It just slipped out – I was just trying to help you, you stupid bastard.

TREVOR. I don't want any fucking help.

MEL. Well, go fuck yourself then, you stupid bastard.

TREVOR. What. (*Threatens MEL with broken chair.*)

MEL. No... Trevor... I didn't mean it. Look, he's gone. It doesn't matter. He can't harm you. They're just jerks, those people, they don't know anything.

TREVOR. It's him or me.

MEL. No, Trevor, it's not like that. Look, if they come round again, let me handle it, Trevor. They're just jerks, those people, I can handle them.

TREVOR sits down.

Look, Trevor, just forget it.

Lights snap down. Hendrix-style guitar music.

ACT TWO

Scene One

TREVOR's *bedsit.*

MEL *and* TREVOR *are playing cards – 'Cheat' – and drinking coffee. It's 1.00 a.m.*

TREVOR. Two fours.

MEL. Three threes.

TREVOR. Two fours.

MEL. Cheat. (*Turns cards over.*) Two fours. (*Picks up cards.*) Hey, Trevor, so you're getting good at this – Hey, wait a minute – what's this fucking jack doing in here? Christ, you really are a slimy bastard when you want to be, aren't you? Come on, play a card.

TREVOR. A nine.

MEL. Hey, what are we gonna do for Christmas?

TREVOR. I don't know.

MEL. Three tens. I had this idea, see – I thought we could go for Christmas dinner to that priest's.

TREVOR. No, I don't want to see that guy again.

MEL. Yeah, but, Trevor, he'd love to see us, we'd get a free meal –

TREVOR. No!

MEL. So who wants to go anyway. Play a card. Come on.

TREVOR. A jack.

MEL. Anyway, Trevor, he's probably forgotten all about it. Doesn't mean anything to him, right? It's just a job. Does it every day. It's probably the most exciting thing that ever happened to him. Four queens.

TREVOR. Cheat.

MEL. What, you calling me a cheat?

TREVOR. Yeah.

MEL (*turns cards over*). One – two – three – four queens.

TREVOR. No, but you put another one down and all –

64

MEL. No, I didn't, Trev –

TREVOR. Yes, you did, cos I put this jack down, and there's another one on top.

MEL. What, you mean this one?

TREVOR. Yeah.

MEL. Jesus, Trevor, I'm sorry, I recognise this card. Don't know how that slipped past me – oh, well – happens to the best of us. Go blank, you know? (*Picks up the rest of the cards.*) All right, Trevor, okay, you can't cheat any more cos I've got all the fucking cards, okay, my boy, you ready for this one? You got to concentrate, Trevor, okay? Four aces. (*Puts down the whole pack.*)

TREVOR. Cheat.

MEL. Yeah…! Hey, Trevor, you know that's the third time you've won one this week. I'd like to shake your hand. Come on – the champion of the Boulevard, the cheat of the street.

They shake hands. MEL *lights a cigarette.*

That's it. No more games. Can't play you any more, Trev, you're too good for me. Hey, tell me something – where'd you learn to play that good? Was it in the nick? Hey, listen, I'm gonna turn in now – I mean, if that's all right with you…

MEL *starts to undress.*

Oh, Trev, I wanna tell you something, I thought you were really great with the priest this morning, you know? Really terrific. You missed the best bit – should've seen his face as he went out the door – it was really beautiful.

TREVOR *is staring.* MEL, *self-conscious, turns her back, unhooks her bra under her T-shirt, and slides it out, and throws it on the bed, i.e. without removing her T-shirt. Takes off her shoes.*

Trevor – where did you put those razor blades?

TREVOR. Under the bed.

MEL. Yeah? How much we gonna charge for them?

TREVOR. About eighteen pee.

MEL. Eighteen? No, Trevor, that's too cheap. People get suspicious. Should be about twenty-five, twenty-six… What do you think?… So, what time do we have to get down there? (*Unzips flies.*)

TREVOR. Market opens about ten o'clock.

MEL. Oh, that means getting up early, right?

She's on the bed, smoking, flies undone. No reaction from
TREVOR. MEL gets up, pulls her trousers down, starts taking
them off.

Hey, Trev – we got rats?

TREVOR. What?

MEL. I said, have we got rats?

TREVOR. Don't know.

MEL. I was just checking. (*Gets into bed with a coffee and a*
cigarette.) Hey, Trev, do you know what they say about the
height of luxury, eh? The height of luxury is supposed to be
sitting in a bath with a bottle of champagne, and a fag. So I
suppose sitting in bed with half a cup of coffee and a fag is
pretty close, wouldn't you say? Ah, this is the life, Trevor.
You should try it… Hey, Trev, how about, you and me
getting a bottle of champagne?

TREVOR. Why?

MEL. We could sit in the sink and celebrate with it… Come on,
can't you picture it, right! – There's you and me and the rats
floating round the sink getting pissed on champagne? Oh
boy, marry a millionaire… yeah…

TREV gets up, bringing ashtray over to the bed.

Hey, where are you going?

TREVOR. I'm bringing this.

MEL. Oh yeah… thank you.

TREVOR (*getting undressed*). I've hurt me foot, you know.

MEL. Yeah? Well, what do you expect if you go round kicking
tables over.

TREVOR gets into bed, MEL sits up.

So what time we getting up then?

TREVOR. Pretty early.

MEL. Will you get me up?

TREVOR. Yeah.

MEL. Oh, wait a minute – Ducker.

She hands him the ashtray which he puts on the floor.

So, what about Christmas dinner – it's all arranged – we're
going to the priest's – okay?

TREVOR. Yeah.

MEL. Good.

She settles down. TREVOR *is still sitting up. She looks at him
one final time, and then turns over. Lights fade.*

In the blackout we hear '1, 2, 3, 4.' Lights up on PHILIP *for
his song – a punkish anthem made up from theme tunes of
TV programmes.*

PHILIP. Boo!
Julie is a wonderful cook, doesn't need a book,
Just reads the back of a frozen pack.
Julie would be a wonderful tart if she didn't – (*Fart noise.*)
Every time in bed till I'm nearly dead.
But the prospect's not that bleak,
I only see her twice a week.
Other days I'm home for tea, when I get in my mother says
    to me:
'Philip, we're off to play bridge,
Your frozen din-dins is in the bleedin' fridge.'

(*Speaking.*) People are funny, aren't they? I know the world
would be a pretty boring place if everyone thought the
same, yes, I know, but what I mean is that it would be nice
if one or two people saw my point of view for a change.
Agreed with me. Take holidays, for instance. This year, Julie
and me – do you remember Julie? She's the one with half a
brain. You know, gifted. Well, we went to Belfast for our
holidays this year. We flew Cunning Lingus. Yes, cos they
fly all the great stars; Glenn Miller, Jim Reeves, Buddy
Holly... We stayed in this nice hotel that she knew, five
pounds a day and meals thrown in – cheap but messy.
Mind you, it was really cold over there. It was so cold I
saw a flasher describing himself. Then I met her mother
and her father – Denise and de nephew, and her anaemic
brother-in-law, Stanley. Oh, anaemic, that's a small
Irishman. What can I say about Stanley? (*Pause.*) Basically,
he wants a kick in the lower falls. Anyway, I said to Julie,
'Belfast wants a bomb dropping on it.' She didn't see my
point of view for a change, did she? She didn't even try.
See, you can please some of the people some of the time;
but you can never please...

(*Singing*.) Julie would be a wonderful wife, a bonus for life,
If she thought again and married Wayne,
Julie and me, would see eye to eye, if she didn't cry
Every time I'm me and she doesn't agree.
And my work is so exciting, when I need a friendly voice,
'I forgot me pill, have you got a sheath,
Your breath's all smelly, have you cleaned your teeth,
Your coughing's getting bad, have you got your spray?
You're very quiet, Philip, are you okay?'
After all I'm not that funny
When all's said and done.
So, I'll tell my jokes to me
Look after number one.

Scene Two

PHILIP *and* JULIE *sit side by side.*

JULIE. Philip, I'd better make arrangements with my parents about coming over. I think they should come by plane. You see, you lose a day if you come by boat. The trouble is it's Daddy. He's terrified of flying. Still, Mummy said she'd get him on it even if she has to give him a few gargles. I'll give them a ring, so I will.

PHILIP. I really fancy a fag, you know, Julie.

JULIE. It's you who wanted the outboard motor, Philip. They should get it cheaper if they book in advance. Oh, I didn't tell you, did I? Denise and the three boys are coming over. Stanley's working, though. It's a pity, isn't it? Cos you and him got on so well together. It's to do with his new job.

PHILIP. I wouldn't mind going and working on that kibbutz for a bit, though, you know.

JULIE. You know I get ill in the heat. Anyway, we've only got two weeks' holiday. Oh, were you there when your parents said that my parents could stop with them? That was very kind of them, wasn't it?

PHILIP. Had a chat with the doctor the other day and he says I've only got three weeks to live.

JULIE. So that means Denise and the three boys can stop in my room with me, cos Maureen said she wouldn't mind moving in with Kathy for the night. Denise said she'd bring a lilo over with her. I'd better get a pump. I'll have a wee word with Mrs McArthy about all this.

PHILIP. I'm going to go out and I'm going to buy a hang-gliding kit.

JULIE. There aren't any hills around here, Philip. Well, I don't think I've forgotten anything. Except you won't forget Friday, will you, Philip?

PHILIP. What?

JULIE. The vicar's! And remember to wear your suit.

PHILIP. I suppose a shag's out of the question?

JULIE. Pardon?

Blackout. Irish-jig linking music.

Scene Three

The vicarage.

PHILIP *and* JULIE *sit on sofa, flanked by* ALEX *and* MEG.

PHILIP. So he's locking up the church last thing at night and he hears this voice saying, 'Mark, Mark', right. So he looks all round the outside of the church. Can't see anyone anywhere. Then, he hears it coming from inside the church, you know, this voice saying, 'Mark, Mark.' Right. Looks all round the inside of the church. Can't find anybody. Then he hears it coming from behind the altar. This voice saying, 'Mark, Mark.' So he looks behind the altar – can't find anybody there, only this dog with a harelip.

Pause.

ALEX. Oh yes! Yes, that's very good, yes. I say, darling, we ought to try that out on the Men's Fellowship. Well now, look, erm, have you thought of a date?

JULIE (*simultaneous*). Yes.

PHILIP (*simultaneous*). No.

ALEX. What?

JULIE. March 17th.

ALEX. March 17th.

69

PHILIP. Possibly.

MEG. A spring wedding – how lovely.

PHILIP. Boring.

ALEX. Darling, would you, um…

MEG. Coffee, anyone? Oh yes.

PHILIP. No thanks, Peg.

JULIE. Yes, please.

ALEX. Er, Meg.

MEG. It's Meg actually. (*To* JULIE.) Sugar?

JULIE. Two please.

PHILIP. Sorry.

MEG (*leaving*). No, no, it's fine.

PHILIP. Peg! That's something you hang your washing up with. Isn't it?

ALEX. Well, I'll make a note of it anyway.

PHILIP. No need, it was just a joke.

ALEX. Now, look, while I think a wedding should be a marvellous party, it is also a major step in both of your lives, and I thi…

PHILIP. Small step for man, giant leap for mankind.

ALEX. Yes, but seriously, Philip, you are taking on major responsibilities, and I suppose my point on your wedding is to put the church's point of view. Because I thin…

PHILIP. Yes, now look, Alec, I hope you don't think this is going to get us going to church every Sunday, cos it isn't.

ALEX. You don't owe me anything. Because you get married in my church, it does not mean I'm going to chase after you and give you a guilty conscience about not coming. Not a bit of it.

PHILIP. Great.

ALEX. My only concern is that your marriage doesn't end up on the scrap heap. Take a moment's thought now, and you can save a lot of 'aggro' later. Take a good hard look at yourselves. You could have all that trouble over alimony, fighting over possession of the kids, breaking up the family home, that sort of thing. Look, put it this way, I'm interested in hundred-per-centers. That means, people who are one hundred per cent sure that they are suited to one another. Then, at least at the outset, the marriage has a decent chance of success.

JULIE. Oh yes, we're sure.

ALEX. Now, there are three main areas where I find marriages go wrong. Firstly the sex life goes up the spout, secondly there are money problems, and the third area is infuriating habits. Now look, I don't know if you two have been in bed together or not, it's none of my business, and I'm not going to delve into it.

PHILIP. Thank you very much.

ALEX. Because when you're married it's because you have a sexual monopoly on one another.

PHILIP. That's a good game, isn't it? I don't think we've played that one.

ALEX. Yes, but you know what I mean, Philip.

PHILIP. No.

ALEX. Well, let's try putting it this way. I suppose in these enlightened days, before you're married, you can more or less sleep round with who you like, but once you're married, you must stick to your partner.

PHILIP. Yes.

ALEX. I mean, it is just the two of you for life.

PHILIP. Oh yes.

ALEX. And I – would suggest that if you haven't already had one, that you have a serious talk about contraception fairly soon. Right?

PHILIP. Right.

ALEX. Money. Now try getting a joint account, because…

JULIE. Oh yes, we have discussed this, haven't we?

ALEX. Fine, okay. Okay. (*Pause.*) Habits.

PHILIP. I don't wear them.

ALEX. When you see somebody three or four evenings a week, or just at the weekends, it is, I promise you, very different from living with them permanently. You suddenly find after about six weeks of marriage…

71

MEG *appears in the doorway with two cups of coffee.*

…that they have these infuriating habits which drive you round the wall. All right, darling, come in, come in.

MEG (*proffering coffee*). Julie. None for Philip. (*To* ALEX.) Darling. (*Sits and starts knitting.*)

PHILIP. How long have you been married then, Alec?

MEG (*simultaneous*). Ten years.

ALEX (*simultaneous*). Ten years.

PHILIP. Ten years?

MEG (*simultaneous*). It's quite a long time, actually.

ALEX (*simultaneous*). It's quite a long time, actually. I mean, I'm not pretending it's all plain sailing.

MEG. No, I think we both feel, don't we, darling… that marriage is something you have to work on…

ALEX (*interrupting*). *Exactly*. It's the way you approach the difficulties that actually makes the difference. If something annoys…

MEG (*to* JULIE). I mean, I think you'll find it's a full-time job, I certainly do.

ALEX. You must, for God's sake, talk about it. Don't bottle things up or you'll blow a gasket. You're bound to have rows, we all have rows. In the end I think it's like Meg says, I think marriage is rather like a garden. It needs constant care and attention to keep it in good shape. It won't look after itself.

PHILIP. Yes, well, she'll be doing all the gardening.

ALEX. Finally, Philip, even if we don't call it in the Christian way, it is the Christian principle that'll help your marriage to become an example of kindness and humanity, and tolerance.

PHILIP (*to* MEG). What are you knitting?

MEG. Dishcloths.

PHILIP. What?

MEG. Dishcloths. I'm raising funds for the CMS.

PHILIP. CMS?

MEG. The Church Missionary Society, I knit so many I'm always saying I get knitter's knuckles, don't I, darling?

ALEX. Yes, that and writer's cramp from doing riddle-me-rees.

MEG. Well, I don't know about that.

PHILIP. Riddle-me-rees. Do you?

MEG. He means riddles, actually. I do riddles and crosswords for the children's page in our magazine, that sort of thing.

PHILIP. Can we hear one then?

MEG. Yes, I don't mind.

JULIE. Did you know that Philip works for the competition page on his newspaper?

MEG. No. You don't, do you, Philip?

PHILIP. Yes.

MEG. Do you really? Gosh. I say, did you know that, darling?

ALEX. No.

PHILIP. Well, let's hear one then.

MEG. Oh no, I couldn't possibly read one of my riddles, it would sound so amateurish to you. But actually if you want to, you're welcome to look at our magazine. I mean, we'd love to have your professional opinion on it. You can even write an article for us if you like.

ALEX. Darling, I'm sure Philip's a very busy man.

PHILIP. No, it's all right. It's just that I don't believe in mixing business and pleasure.

MEG. Yes, no, of course, quite wise.

PHILIP (*simultaneous*). Well, I think...

ALEX (*simultaneous*). Have you seen the...

MEG (*simultaneous*). I was going to say...

ALEX. No, no, I was just going to say have you seen the inside of the church.

JULIE. No.

ALEX. Where it's all going to take place. Now look, any time you want to, just feel free. Because in our church the door's never, ever locked, it's always open.

PHILIP. Things get stolen, Alec.

MEG. No, they don't. Not in our church – everything's already been stolen.

ALEX. It's just that I happen to believe that a church door should never, ever be locked; oh, I don't know, you may have read about it. A couple of months ago, in the paper, I had this 'Keep Our Churches Open' campaign going.

PHILIP. KOCO.

ALEX. Sorry?

PHILIP. KOCO.

ALEX. Darling, could you…

MEG. Yes, yes, anything.

PHILIP. No, no, Keep – Our – Churches…

MEG (*squawks*). C – O – C – O – A.

ALEX. Yes, yes, yes, yes, yes.

MEG. Oh, darling, isn't that clever? You should have thought of that.

PHILIP. Yes, well, that's…

MEG. Well done, Philip, that's awfully clever.

PHILIP. Well…

MEG. You can see where he gets that job from. He's got one of those marvellous quick brains.

PHILIP. Yes, well… You like your cocoa, do you, Alex?

ALEX (*laughing*). Well, funnily enough, I do, actually.

MEG (*laughing*). As a matter of fact, he does. You know, just before bed.

They all laugh except JULIE.

PHILIP. God. (*Pause.*) Actually, Alec, you seem a bit of a rebel to me.

MEG. Oh yes, Alex is quite outspoken.

ALEX. Well, I get told to keep my mouth shut now and then.

MEG. Actually, you know, Philip, he's quite famous for his outrageous sermons. As a matter of fact, they'd appeal to you. You ought to come along and have a listen one Sunday.

ALEX. Darling, I was trying to explain, we're not trying to force Philip into anything just at the moment.

MEG. I just thought he might find your sermons interesting, that's all.

ALEX. Yes, I suppose as a casual observer you might like to trot along one Sunday and have a listen.

PHILIP. Yes, I think we better had – be trotting along, I mean.

JULIE. Philip, I want to find out about costs; could you tell me how much it'll cost me, please.

ALEX. Well, as far as the church service itself goes, it's just £7.50, which is my fee, which keeps us in bread and butter, and we hope we might get a free meal at the reception afterwards.

JULIE. Oh, I was going to ask you about that. I've budgeted for £3.50 a head. Do you think that's reasonable?

MEG. Yes, that's plenty.

ALEX. Fine, fine, as long as you don't drink vintage champagne or anything.

MEG. Have you thought where you're going to have your reception?

JULIE. No, but I've written to some places and they're going to send menus on.

MEG. Oh, that's a good idea.

ALEX. A word of warning – whatever you do, don't go to The Tibworth.

JULIE. Oh, no?

ALEX. No. It's dreadful – quite appalling. I always say they'd have cancelled the Last Supper if they'd cooked it in there.

JULIE *and* ALEX *laugh.*

Now, Philip, as for the music, it's all free. Now, you can either have the parish group – they're not exactly The Rolling Stones but not bad. Or, I suppose, more traditionally you can stick with the organ, or if you're feeling really adventurous, you might have a bash at the string quartet.

MEG. You know, we had a string quartet at our wedding.

JULIE. I think I prefer the organ.

PHILIP. She always does.

MEG. Yes, I like the organ too – beautiful instrument.

Slow fade. Irish-jig linking music.

75

Scene Four

PHILIP*'s car.*

PHILIP. Do you want to go for a drink? (*Pause.*) Pardon? Do you want to drink? Julie? (*Pause.*) What's the matter? Oh, Christ!

JULIE. What do you think's the matter with me, Philip?

PHILIP. What?

JULIE. I suppose you think there's nothing wrong. Is that it? Is it?

PHILIP. What.

JULIE. Do you know, I've never been so embarrassed in all my life.

PHILIP. What are you talking about?

JULIE. What were you doing, Philip?

PHILIP. What?

JULIE. What do you mean, 'What'!

PHILIP. What?

JULIE. When he asked us about the date.

PHILIP. We haven't decided about the date.

JULIE. Yes, we have.

PHILIP. No, you haven't.

JULIE. Yes, we have. We decided, we discussed it together.

PHILIP. You discussed it.

JULIE. We decided on March.

PHILIP. Maybe.

JULIE. You treated me as if I didn't know what I was talking about.

PHILIP *laughs.*

Don't you laugh at me, do you hear? You made me feel a fool and I won't put up with it, and I won't stand for it, do you hear me?

PHILIP (*interrupts*). Just let me say this; you were talking for both of us in there.

JULIE. You were embarrassing those good people in there.

PHILIP. How do you know?

76

JULIE. Ack! You're not human. You and your stupid jokes. They're not even funny. Nobody was laughing at your jokes. Nobody wanted to hear your jokes.

PHILIP *impersonates Jimmy Saville.*

Oh, who are you being now, Philip. Come on, who is it? If you're so funny then make me laugh. (*Pause.*) Philip, I'm not laughing. Trouble is, I don't know who you are. Oh, come on; what were you trying to prove in there? Can you never talk to anyone without taking the rise out of them? Can you never be serious? I'll tell you one thing, Philip, things had better change because if they don't, what is the point of us getting married?

PHILIP. You're funny, very funny. You'll be a riot down at the hospital. (*Pats* JULIE's *cheek.*)

JULIE. Take your hand away from my face. (*Pushes him away – slight struggle.*) Agh, who are you being now? I think I know this one, Philip. It's the Statue of Liberty. Who are you, Philip? You're nothing. You know that. You're just nothing.

PHILIP. Give us a kiss.

JULIE. Philip, I'm not playing games. Why is it you've always got to play games, Philip, why?

Long pause.

PHILIP (*has an asthma attack throughout this*). It's the way I tell 'em. (*Pause.*) It's a cracker this, isn't it. You see, you're all the same. On and on and on. And him... 'Rolling Stones'. (*Pause.*) Pardon? (*Has attack.*)

Gradually JULIE *melts, takes* PHILIP's *hand and puts her head on his shoulder. He smiles. Fade out.*

The ENTIRE COMPANY *perform 'The Bells Go Hey!', as much as possible like the Irish entry for the Eurovision Song Contest.*

In the power of my devotion what comes singing through?
In the light of my emotion what comes shining through?
It's the S in your smile
When you walk down the aisle,
It's the G in your grace,
It's the love in your face,
Well the bells go hey ding a ding a ding hey,
The bells go ding for you,
And the song I sing hey ding a ding a ding, babe,

The song I sing to you,
And my heart takes wing, hey wing a wing hey, babe,
My heart takes wing for you,
When I give you the ring, hey ring a ring ring, babe,
When I give the ring to you.
Ding dong ding dong ding dong ding dong.

Scene Five

TREVOR's *bedsit.*

MEL *reading a comic. Knock at the door.* MEL *opens it.*

MEL. Oh, Mrs Bridie – hello.

MEG. Hello, Mel – can I come in?

MEL. Oh, yeah, sure, why not? Trevor's not here. He's at the betting shop.

MEG. Oh, really. Ah, well, as a matter of fact, Mel, I thought I'd pop in and see you anyway – because I felt sure I saw you yesterday, on the market.

MEL. Oh, really.

MEG. Yes. As a matter of fact I waved. I tried to catch you up. I thought perhaps we could all have a coffee together or something like that.

MEL. That's very nice of you, Mrs Bridie.

MEG. But then I lost you in the crowd. Didn't you see me?

MEL. Well, you know, we saw someone waving madly, and we thought 'Oh, it must be Mrs Bridie,' but we weren't sure, so...

MEG. I thought you'd got yourself a job on the market.

MEL. What do you mean, 'a job'?

MEG. Well, I thought perhaps you were standing in front of a box.

MEL. Oh no, you see, Mrs Bridie, we went down there to meet someone, but he didn't turn up...

MEG. Oh, I thought you were selling something, you see.

MEL. Oh no. Well, look, Mrs Bridie, you might have seen us standing in front of a box.

MEG. Yes, yes, I did…

MEL. Yes, well, there are lots of boxes in the market.

MEG. Of course. How are things?

MEL. Oh, all right, same as usual. What was it round about?

MEG. Yes, well, obviously, Mel, the real reason I came round is because I want to try and clear things up after the fracas of the other day…

MEL. After the what?

MEG. After what went on between you two and my husband, you see I feel slightly responsible –

MEL. Oh, that, oh, that's nothing, Mrs Bridie. I mean, I'd forget it if I was you, cos we have.

MEG. Well, I don't think it could have been nothing, Mel, because as a matter of fact I've been told not to come round here any more.

MEL. Oh yeah?

MEG. Yes, as a matter of fact my husband said if I came round here I'd get murdered. But you see I do feel responsible for what happened because as you know I went home and spilled the beans, as it were, but then, you see, Mel, when you're married it doesn't occur to you to keep secrets from your partner…

MEL. Yeah, well, I wouldn't know about that…

MEG. It's almost as though you're one and the same person, if you see what I mean, and my husband is such a sincere man and he takes his job very seriously.

MEL. Excuse me, Mrs Bridie, do you mind if I say something here?

MEG. No, yes, please.

MEL. Right now, you see, Mrs Bridie, what happened when he came round here was his fault.

MEG. Whose?

MEL. The priest's.

MEG. We don't call him a priest, Mel.

MEL. Well, what do you call him?

MEG. We call him a vicar.

79

MEL. Yeah, well, that's one thing you could call him, I suppose.

MEG. Yes, I suppose in a way you're right, Mel. It was his fault. But you see when you're as nice a man as that and you take your job that seriously.

MEL. Mrs Bridie, he is not sincere. He came round shooting his mouth off cos someone messed about with his precious religion.

MEG. As a matter of fact, Mel, he is sincere, and he's very concerned about you two.

MEL. I'm sure he's very concerned but he should aim to keep religion inside the church, right? Where it belongs. Not go poking his nose into other people's business cos we don't want it.

MEG. Ah, well, that's where you're wrong, you see, Mel, because we have no intention of poking our noses into your private affairs. Quite frankly, Mel, as far as I'm concerned, all that worries me is the relationship I've built up with Trevor. I mean, surely even you can understand, I don't want that to 'go for a Burton', do I?

MEL. No. Even I can understand that, Mrs Bridie.

MEG. Mel, why don't you tell me about this 'black magic' business…?

MEL. There's nothing to tell.

MEG. I mean to say, what exactly is it that Trevor believes in?

MEL. How do I know, Mrs Bridie? I don't know.

MEG. Well, you must know. You live with him.

MEL. So what? Look, Mrs Bridie, I don't ask him any questions, you see, cos it's none of my business.

MEG. Are you in love with him?

MEL. With who?

MEG. Trevor.

MEL (*laughs*). Why, are you?

MEG. *No!*

Enter TREVOR.

MEL. Oh. Talk of the devil. Hello, Trevor.

MEG. Hello, Trevor.

MEL. Been down the betting shop, have you?

MEG. Did you back any winners?

MEL. Oh, Trev. She saw us in the market yesterday. When we were waiting for Frank, remember?

MEG. Yes, Trevor. As a matter of fact, I waved and tried to catch you up – I thought we might all have a coffee together, but then I lost you in the crowd. Did you see me?

TREVOR. No.

MEG. Ah. Any job news?

MEL. Trevor, she wants to apologise for what happened between you and her husband...

MEG. Yes, Trevor. I'm afraid my husband's rather upset.

MEL. Oh, he's rather upset. Why?

MEG. He feels he's failed. Look, Trevor, as far as I'm concerned I just hope this isn't going to ruin everything. I mean to say you will still be doing the Christmas decorations, won't you?

MEL. Well, go on, answer the lady. Are you going to do them or what? Mrs Bridie, we're coming round for Christmas dinner anyway, so we'll see you there.

TREVOR. No, we're not. No.

MEL. What do you mean? We decided it the other night when we...

TREVOR. I've changed me mind.

MEL. What do you mean, you've changed your mind?

TREVOR. Leave it.

MEG. Look, Trevor, are you all right for everything? I mean, do you need any money or clothes or blankets...

MEL. No, Trev, listen, she thinks you're upset about what happened but you can see he's not upset, Mrs Bridie...

MEG. Look, Trevor, don't you feel that after all this time, I mean, and after the friendship we've built up that it would be a crying shame if just because of a trivial incident that happened here the other day between you two and my husband...

TREVOR. Look, I don't want to see that guy again.

81

MEG. No, of course no, Trevor. But you must understand that he didn't mean you any harm, I mean, you know as well as I...

MEL. Look, Mrs Bridie, he's just said he doesn't want to see... What?

MEG (*staring at* MEL). Thank you. Trevor, you know as well as I do that my husband's an emotional man and he felt it was his job, rightly or wrongly, to ask you about your private life. I mean, surely you can understand that?

TREVOR. I'm not answering any questions.

MEG. No, of course not, Trevor, and I'm not here to ask you any questions. All I want you to understand is that sometimes people get carried away.

MEL. Look, Mrs Bridie, it's just his fucking attitude.

TREVOR. Shut up.

MEG. All right, Trevor, do you want me to leave –

MEL. Look, Trevor, I'm on your side –

MEG. I mean to say surely all this can be patched up. I mean to say that my husband is only out for your good and that he means you no harm –

MEL. Mrs Bridie, I'm trying to say something. Trevor, I want you to listen...

MEL *sets light to parish magazine.*

...to this. She's got it into her tiny mind that I'm in love with you. So what do you think about that, Mrs Bridie.

TREVOR. What the fuck are you doing?

MEL. What?

MEG. Look, Trevor, you must understand that basically we're not interested in your private life. I mean to say, what you do in your private life...

TREVOR (*leaving*). Oh no, I'm not staying here.

MEG. No, wait a minute, Trevor, just wait a minute...

MEL. You're not going to let her drive you out, are you...?

TREVOR. Look, I don't want any of this fucking interference. Why don't you fuck off. (*Goes.*)

MEL. Well, you made a good job of that one, didn't you, Mrs Bridie?

MEG (*putting out burning parish magazine*). Look, Mel, if you go on being negative all your life, we'll never be able to help people like Trevor.

MEL. He doesn't need your help.

MEG. After all, he's just as much yours as mine.

MEL. He's what?

MEG. Well, you are lovers.

MEL. You just keep on talking, Mrs Bridie, cos that's what you're good at.

MEG. Look, Mel, you must understand that I've no quarrel with you, we're equally concerned, if you did but know it.

MEL. 'Concern.' Wait a minute, that's not my word. I'm not concerned. I don't give a fuck about other people. Other people, just fuck 'em.

MEG. I realise you only talk like this to shock. And you do care about other people.

MEL. Oh yeah, I'm like you, right. I mean, you love everybody, everybody loves you…

MEG. I'm not saying I love everybody, but the least we can do in this life is make some attempt.

MEL. The least you can do, Mrs Bridie, is fill it up with a load of fucking useless crap. I know, see, because I've met people like you before.

MEG. I think you've met the wrong ones, Mel.

MEL. Do you?

MEG. Look, I've got to go now. Is there anything you need?

MEL. No.

MEG. Well, I'll pop in next week to make sure. All right? Goodbye, Mel.

Fade.

MEG's song (*in the style of Kurt Weill*).

I've got to make some shortbread and a couple of cakes
For this afternoon's meeting of the mother's union,
And fry some bacon and two or three eggs
For Alex's breakfast when he gets back from communion;
Mrs Green's collecting for spastics I mustn't forget to thank
    her,

And remind her that she's going to be included in the
    knitting list for dishcloths to Sri Lanka.
I've got to launder the cassocks
And organise someone to polish the pews,
I think we need some new hassocks
But I don't know what colour to choose.
No, I don't know what colour to choose.
And I think that they ought to be blue,
Cos I'm feeling a little blue too.
No, I don't think they ought to be red,
My marriage is just about...
I've got to concoct a riddle-me-ree
For the children's page in the parish magazine.
I've got to go shopping but I can't have the car
Cos Alex says he needs it for his meeting with the dean;
And he wants me to type out a pamphlet
About a dynamic new creed for the people,
And organise a meeting which will organise a way
Of raising funds to save the steeple.
There's a meeting after bingo at the Thursday Club
And I said I would supply the prize,
And it seems to me about a decade
Since I gazed into Alex's eyes,
Since I gazed into Alex's eyes.
And I think that they ought to be blue,
Cos I'm feeling a little blue too.
And my eyes, oh my eyes are red,
Cos my marriage is just about...

Scene Six

TREVOR's *bedsit.*

TREVOR *is standing by the door.* MEL *is sat at the far side of the table.*

MEL. Look, Trev, I didn't tell her anything, right. I just told her to fuck off. She doesn't know anything.

TREVOR. Neither do you, do you?

MEL. Look, Trevor, just don't take it out on me, right. Look, Trevor, come on, what's the matter with you? Can't you see the joke? Are you pissed? All right, Trevor, come on. I'll tell you everything. All right? Come on, sit down – I'll tell you everything I said if you just sit down. Oh, for Christ's sake! All right, stand up if you want. You do what the fuck you like. Cos I don't care.

TREVOR. I will.

MEL. Trevor, this is really getting on my nerves. Hey, Trevor, tell me – where do they live?

TREVOR. Why?

MEL. Why? I don't know – she got me so mad when she came round here this afternoon, I had this idea, see. I'm gonna chuck a brick through her window.

TREVOR. Well, you're mad. They'd get the police, wouldn't they?

MEL. Trevor, they will not get the police! They're church people. Look, what are you so scared of – hey? Oh Christ, she's really got a hold of you, hasn't she?

TREVOR. It's not them.

MEL. No? Well, what is it then, Trev? Are you all right? Hey, listen, have a cigarette. C'mon. Have one of mine… come on.

He comes over slowly and sits at the table. MEL *hands him a cigarette and lights it for him.*

(*NB Hereafter he pays no attention to the cigarette.*)

Look, Trevor, do you want to talk about it? Look, you don't have to talk about it if you don't want to. I mean, I'm not going to push you – cos I'm not like her. So… what's it all about, then?

TREVOR. It's all about everything… I feel funny… I've got information, y'see.

MEL. What information?

TREVOR. Well, I hear things… people… see – I know what's going to happen.

MEL. What, you mean, to you?

TREVOR. No.

MEL. Well, what then? Trevor, I don't know what you're talking about.

TREVOR. A lot of people are going to die.

MEL. Yeah? Including you, right?

TREVOR. No.

MEL. No? Look, Trevor, if it isn't gonna happen to you, it doesn't matter, right. What are you worrying about other people for? It's not your problem.

TREVOR. Blacks and that.

MEL. Wait a minute. You mean just blacks?

TREVOR. No. All the fucking deadweight, right. All the fucking deadweight on the world that's bringing it down. Fucking gonna die. Like blacks… and businessmen. All kinds… Lee Harvey Oswald told me. I know all about the Kennedy murder, I do.

MEL. Trevor, everybody knows about the Kennedy murder. You can read it anywhere. It was the CIA? Right?

TREVOR. No. It was Heaven.

MEL. What?

TREVOR. The Klansmen – er – the Klansmen from Heaven. They killed him – to get him on their side. And they killed Martin Luther King and all to get him on their side.

MEL. No, Trevor, they wouldn't want Martin Luther King cos he's black, right.

TREVOR. Not any more he isn't… And they give me these words to say. Cos I'm on their side. 'Murder losers, Klansmen'… And… 'Join forces, Klansmen.' It's initials.

MEL. You believe all that, do you, Trevor? Eh? Trevor, even if it is true, so what? It doesn't matter. Listen, Trev, I know; we'll go down to the *News of the World* and sell it to them. We'll make a bomb on it… No, seriously, listen, Trev. I had this dream, see, I had this dream that Nelson Rockefeller ruled the world. Do you believe that? Trevor, did you meet any nutters in prison?

TREVOR. There's only one man in the world knows about this.

MEL. Yeah? Who's that?

TREVOR. Johnny Cash.

MEL. Johnny Cash.

She notices that TREVOR *is no longer aware of what is happening. She collects her bag and coat and exits, watching* TREVOR *all the time.*

Fade out.

MEL*'s song.*

Don't tell me about the right ways of living,
All this love and forgiving,
Cos it don't get you nowhere.
I can do without social analysing,
Comprising, I'm realising,
It's the fool in the shrink's chair.
Cos my life is okay and I'll be moving on my way.
Don't need any love-thy-neighbour concern,
Will they ever learn
That God helps nobody,
It's a con, won't be long
Before you're not so strong
And bam! They've got you,
That ain't for me
Cos my life is okay and I'll be moving on my way.
I had a dream
I was running.
The Mafia were gunning for me,
And the driver's girl was Sophia Loren,
And the Pope at the wheel of a pink Cadillac,
It's at my back.
Hope it's not too late to make my escape,
Heading down to Sicily,
What do I see?
Nothing but plasticine in the sea,
And I'm locked in a room,
The Mafia say 'Get her where it hurts with a knife',
And I start to pray,
'Oh my God, make the vision go',
And you know what?
God said 'No.'
So don't come on with that crap about religion,
Supervision, make decisions for me,
That won't change me.
I can handle it alone, nothing to moan about,
You're on your own, brother, so
Don't rearrange me.
Cos my life is okay and I'll be moving on my way.
Look, I don't think I'm asking a lot,
Just a question of not trying to judge me,
You're wise when you can see that nothing flatters.

Nothing matters, if you're battered,
(*Laugh.*) Nothing can touch me.
Cos my life is okay and I'll be moving on my way.
I'm moving on my way.
Yes, my life is okay,
I'm moving on my way, okay.

Scene Seven

The vicarage.

ALEX *seated.* MEG *enters.*

MEG. Hello, darling.

ALEX. Hello.

MEG. All right?

ALEX. Yes.

MEG. You seem rather quiet. (*Pause.*) I called on Trevor. Well, I knew it would be all right. I knew they wouldn't attack me. Really it was all right. Do you see? They didn't mind me being there. (*Pause.*) He said he didn't want to be interfered with. Then he went out again. He wasn't actually in a bad temper. I think he'd lost some money on the horses or something like that. We had quite a good chat, she and I. She said she wasn't selling anything on the market yesterday. She said she was just meeting Trevor. And she said she thought she saw me. I don't think they were doing anything illegal. (*Pause.*) She set fire to our magazine. I think she was trying to frighten me so I didn't take any notice. (*Pause.*) Do you want to hear any more? (*Pause.*) He doesn't want to see you again. I said we weren't trying to interfere in their private lives but she disagreed. She said they didn't want any help. But then she's too young. She doesn't know. She said she didn't need people, but obviously she needs people because she's living with Trevor. They are lovers. (*Pause.*) I think I'll go back. I think it'll all blow over. (*Pause.*) Look, I simply said you were hurt...

ALEX. Meg...

MEG. And ups[et]...

ALEX. Meg, please. Please don't say anything else.

Pause.

MEG. I'm sorry.

ALEX. I'm going to the church. (*Gets up and goes to the door.*)

MEG. Alex. Alex, please come back.

He goes out. Fade. Chinese linking music into phone-call positions.

Scene Eight

PHILIP *and* WAYNE *on either side of the stage.*

WAYNE (*Chinese accent*). 'Herro'…

PHILIP. 'Herro'…

WAYNE. 'One-Long-Bang'…

PHILIP. 'Good heaving, heavy body.' How are you, matey?

WAYNE. Fine. Eh, listen, what are you doing a week on Saturday?

PHILIP. A week on Saturday. Em, skiing up Mount Everest, I think. Why?

WAYNE. Me and Pam are getting married.

PHILIP. Oh yes, really.

WAYNE. Yeah, really.

Pause.

PHILIP. What, really?

WAYNE Yeah!

PHILIP (*laughs*). Good God. Why?

WAYNE. Well…

PHILIP. You've not been a naughty boy, have you, Wayne, forgotten to go to the chemist? Wayne.

WAYNE. What?

PHILIP. You've not, have you?

Pause.

WAYNE. Well…

PHILIP. Oh, you stupid bugger, Wayne. You want a permanent wave putting in it.

WAYNE. Look, you've got to do the right thing. We'd wanted to ask you if you'd like to be the witness.

PHILIP. Will anyone who saw the accident…

WAYNE. It's a registry-office do. You can wear your three-piece suite if you like. Can you make it?

PHILIP. Yes.

WAYNE. Oh, great. I'll see you there then.

PHILIP. Yes.

WAYNE. Well, cheers then.

PHILIP. Cheers, Wayne.

Fade.

Scene Nine

The pulpit.

ALEX *enters. Playover music: 'All People that On Earth Do Dwell'.*

ALEX. Good morning. It's nice to see you all. Next Sunday will be the second Sunday in Advent. Holy Communion will be at 8.30, the family service at eleven o'clock, and it's Sung Evensong next Sunday at 6.30. I publish the banns of marriage between Philip de Berger, bachelor of St Mary's of Beverley, and Julie Jane Carson, spinster of this parish. If any of you know cause or just impediment why these two persons should not be joined together in holy matrimony, ye are to declare it. This is the first time of asking. In the name of the Father, the Son and the Holy Ghost, Amen.

This is Dr Sheila Cassidy writing in the *Observer* about the torture she received at the hands of the Chilean Fascists: 'They secured me to the bottom half of the bunk, tying my wrists and ankles and upper arms and placing a wide band across my chest and abdomen. I felt an electric shock pass through me, then another and another. One electrode was placed in my vagina and the other, a wandering pincer, was used to stimulate me wherever they chose. The pain was appalling and so they broke me. I felt sick with humiliation at my betrayal. I said to the man who sat beside me, "Does everyone talk or am I weak?" He replied "Everyone has their breaking point." ' Everyone has their breaking point. Last week I was sitting at home, having a cup of coffee, writing at my desk – there was a loud crash and a brick came through the window. I didn't run out into the street to see who it was, or phone the police – I didn't have to. I just accepted the fact that there was a brick on my carpet. You see, it represented for me a failure, a total inability to cope with something within my parish. I felt bitter. I felt alone, I even questioned my faith. You see, I felt like Dr Cassidy – appalled at the thought of having betrayed my work and the Christian principles that I believe in and that I stand for. I thought how easy it would be to go back to Africa, where the results are so *easy* to see. But that would be a soft option, and I think I'm needed here, needed in this parish, where the Devil is so difficult to locate, where the visible results of my work are so, so elusive. And – well, I think anyway – that Christianity isn't a soft option. I think it's a fight. I think it's a fight to make our world the sort of place where Christ wouldn't be shoved in the loony bin on Valium. A fight to replace those Chilean fascists with liberals. A fight to replace the bigoted with the enlightened, the prejudiced with the open-minded. We are bound to suffer setbacks, and when the electrodes are strapped to our bodies, it is time for self-examination certainly, but it is no time for the faint-hearted. When we reach the breaking point it is merely a platform for a new assault on the evils around us, time for a new commitment to Christ. That is a hard – and a long – and often lonely path to tread, and it's… it's when we read such almost unbelievably horrific accounts as Dr Cassidy's – it's when we realise just how far there is to go.

Then teach us, good Lord, to serve Thee as Thou deservest. To give and not to count the cost. To fight and not to heed the wounds. To toil and not to seek for rest. To labour, and not to look for any reward save that of knowing that we do Thy will. And may the words of my mouth and the thoughts of all our hearts be now and always acceptable in Thy sight, O Lord, my strength and my redeemer, Amen.

The COMPANY *enter to sing one verse of 'Hand in Hand' and then sing the last few bars of 'All We Like Sheep' from Handel's Messiah – 'And the Lord hath laid on him the iniquity of us all'.*

Song.

ALL.
    Hand in hand,
    Hand in hand,
    From land to land,
    Brothers and sisters,
    Hand in hand.

    And the Lord hath laid on him the iniquity of us all.

Curtain.

The End.

Blinding Gloucester

Working with a Text

After ten years of devised plays I went back to working with writers, and I found myself adapting the devised character work to texts.

In a devised play you work with the actors individually to create characters that will end up in the play. With a text you take the characters out of the play and then work out how they got there and why they behave like they do.

And as always the first question is:

Who Am I?

As an actor it is impossible to get inside anybody else's head. We only have ourselves to work from and must use our imagination to create other versions of ourselves who can then tell the stories that the playwrights want to tell.

Similarly, there are a million different ways that an actor can play any part. The character-building process determines which one of these million other selves they are going to be. The director's function is to help them make their mind up.

The place to start is always the text itself. An actor must 'mine the text' and search for clues:

- What does my character do?
- What does my character say?
- What happens to my character?
- What do other people say about my character?

In addition, the actor must find any reference to the character and any other suggestions that the playwright may have to offer. With new plays it's quite usual to have the writer in the rehearsal room, and so they can provide information about how the character evolved. This often provides insights not readily obvious from the text.

It also helps if the actor writes out the story of the play seen exclusively from the character's point of view. After all, the characters do not have the luxury of having read the play and often don't have all the information that the other characters or indeed the audience have. As a director I repeat the same procedure, but for all the characters in the play, so if we have six characters I have to study the six different versions of the play from the six different perspectives.

To illustrate the process I am going to use the character of Peter from Jack Thorne's play *When You Cure Me,* which I directed at the Bush in 2005.

From Jack's *dramatis personae* we find out that Peter is seventeen and that the play is set in Reading over a period of three months between January and March, and the time is roughly the present. So we have to mine the text for the story and for clues. And this is what we find:

PETER is seventeen and an only child. He lives with his mother, his father having disappeared several years ago. Peter's mother has a history of mental illness and Peter has participated in her therapy sessions. He is nervous and shy but very bright and good at football. He's the one who does the cleaning up after the party and is nice to everyone's mum. He lives on the same estate as James and Rachel. At the time of the play he has been going out with Rachel for six months. They were both virgins when they met. Peter and James have been best friends for years although Peter tends to play second fiddle. He has fancied James's girlfriend Alice for years but knows she is out of his league. He has asthma and uses an inhaler at times of stress. Peter, Rachel, James and Alice all go to the same school. Before the play opens, Rachel has been attacked and raped. She has developed psychosomatic paralysis and is now bedridden. Peter doesn't know what to do. He wants to help, but has no idea how. At school, however, his status changes – he has become the target for unfettered sympathy.

So these are the building blocks we have to go on to create the actor's individual version of Peter.

At this point, readers might like to read the play (which is printed at the end of this book) and see if you come to the same conclusions.

Building the Character

I often start by asking actors if they can think of anybody, or indeed combinations of people, that they know who resemble the character in any way. It can be quite useful to think of people that they were at school with and imagine if that person could have become the character. This is not to say that the actor is going to end up playing Peter as an impersonation of their chum Eric Boocock; it's just a way of finding a target, someone to aim for. My character Norman in Mike Leigh's film *Bleak Moments* was roughly inspired by someone I knew who used to go to Scunthorpe Folk Club.

The next step is to construct a life history of the character based on what we have discovered from the text, but also inventing our own detail.

In the case of Peter we know that he is seventeen, so we have seventeen years to fill up to the start of the play. The easiest way to start is with a basic timeline, adding significant events along the way.

If the play is set in 2005 then Peter was born in 1987 thus:

1987	Born in Slough. Mother Anne aged twenty-three. Father Brian aged twenty-four. Peter first and only child. Brian works at Honeywell Computers. Anne gives up work at health centre.
1988	Father promoted. Gets new car.
1989	Family moves to Reading.
1990	Family holiday in Cornwall.
1991	
1992	
1993	Primary school.
1994	
1995	
1997	Father leaves home. Mother has breakdown. Develops asthma.
1998	Primary-school football team.
1999	
2000	Secondary school: Maiden Erlegh Comprehensive, Reading. Meets best friend James.
2001	Wins school history prize.
2002	First girlfriend. Gets drunk.
2003	
2004	Seventeenth birthday. Passes GCSEs. Goes into sixth form. Starts dating Rachel.
2005	Rachel attacked. *Play begins.*

Starting with this very rough route map, I work with each actor individually, creating the character's life history starting from when they were born up to the time they enter the play. It's a very detailed and painstaking process and I have, over the years, devised a series of visualisation exercises that seem to help the actors to find their characters.

Life-History Visualisation Exercises

The idea is that the actors create images of the life story of their character in their imagination. They should try to see it in pictures; it should be like playing the movie in their head. I ask a series of rhetorical questions and the actor conjures up images based on those questions. They don't respond out loud. Equally, they don't have to come up with answers for everything and should let their imagination take them wherever it wants to go. Inevitably an actor will rifle their own memories and fantasies and adapt them to chime with the biography of the character. This is fine. It helps if the actors close their eyes.

Characters Aged Nought to Five
We start with very small people:

> Where were you born? And when? (So what's your birth sign?) Can you picture your mother? And your father? Do you have any older brothers and sisters? What was the first house you lived in? What did it look like? Was it in the town or the country? Did it have a garden? What did your father do for a living? And your mother? Was it a noisy house? Were there aunts and uncles, cousins, grandparents? Did the family have a car? Did you have a pet? Did you have a television, a music centre, a computer? Did you have a nanny, a babysitter, a childminder? Who were they and what did they look like? (Play the movie in your head...) Did anyone read to you? And what did they read? Did you watch cartoons? Did you go to Sunday school? Did you say your prayers? Who did

you play with? Who was your best friend? Did you go on holidays? Did you go to pre-school, playgroup, kindergarten? Were you ill? Did you get mumps, measles, chickenpox? Did you go to hospital? Can you think of an activity you did solely with your mother? And with your father? Did you paint, draw? Did anyone teach you to read? Were you ever punished? Were you hit? Did you go to dance classes? Did you learn a musical instrument? Did you like dressing up? Were you scared of the dark? Did you believe in fairies? Did you go to a wedding or a funeral? Did you get any younger brothers and sisters? Did you know anybody who died? Did you tell a lie? (Play the movie in your head…)

Now, these may look like a bunch of totally arbitrary questions, but in fact they are loaded to cover as much ground as possible in a short space of time and to provide a platform on which to build the character.

Characters Aged Five to Eight

As the characters grow older, the questions change to emphasise different aspects, such as friends, school and interests.

What was the first school you went to? What did it look like? How did you get there? Did anyone take you there? Did you know anyone at school? What was your favourite subject? What subject did you like least? (I have never come across an actor whose character liked maths.) Who was your favourite teacher? Were you in a gang? Who were your friends? What did you do together? Was it a mixed school? Who did you know of the opposite sex? Did you play Kiss-Chase, Doctors and Nurses, Cowboys and Indians? Who did you play with? What was your favourite toy? Did you have a hobby? Did you play sports? Were you in a team? Were you precocious at chess? What was your favourite book? Did you have friends to sleep over? Did you have birthday parties?

Were you bullied? Did you do any bullying? Did you have nickname? Did you keep a diary? What did you do exclusively with your mother? And your father? Did you go to church? Did you say your prayers? What do you want to be when you grew up? Did you have a favourite pop star? What was your favourite TV show? When did you find out about 'the Facts of Life' and who told you? And did you believe them? Did you know any dirty jokes? Had you come across racism? Had you seen a ghost? Did you move house? Did you get any younger brothers and sisters? Where did you go on holiday? What did you get for Christmas? How much pocket money did you get? What did you spend it on? Have you been to a wedding or a funeral? Do you know anybody who has died? Had you been abroad? What did your bedroom look like? (Play the movie in your head...)

Again, the questions are loaded to illuminate aspects of the character's background. For example, a character who has suffered from bullying is a very different person from the one who has been doing the bullying.

If I were conducting this exercise with the actor playing Peter, I would ask questions that would focus on the fact that his father left when Peter was eight. Imagining the circumstances of his departure and the subsequent effect this had on Peter's mother would help to unlock the scene in which Peter tells Rachel of his experience with therapy.

Characters Aged Eight to Ten

Did you move house? Did you go to a new school? Did you have a school uniform? How did you get on with your parents? What did you like doing at school and what did you dislike? What was your best subject? Did you sing? Were you in the school play? Did you believe in God? Did you have a boyfriend or a girlfriend? Did you get any Valentine's cards? Did you have a kiss? Were you in a gang? Did you have a nickname? Were you ever bullied? Did you do any bullying? Were you ill? Did you go in hospital? Did you smoke a cigarette? Did you try alcohol? Were you in trouble? Did you get punished? Did you steal anything? What was the worst swear word in the world? Did you have homework? Did you do your homework? Did you have extra tuition? Did you take any exams? Who was your best friend? Did you have any heroes or heroines? Did you have to do household chores? Did you have a pet? Were you a Boy Scout or a Brownie? Who bought your clothes? Did you choose them yourself? Were you ever in detention? Did you go abroad? Did you watch the news? Did you read a newspaper? How did your parents vote? Did you ever see your parents row? How did you get on with your brothers and sisters? Did you believe in flying saucers? Did you know anyone who died? Were you in love? What did you want to be when you grow up?

As you can see, a number of questions are repeated in each age group to chart the shifts in thought, experience and opinions of the character.

The questions also reflect the character's educational progress.

Characters Aged Ten to Thirteen

Did you go to a new school? What was that like? Were you frightened? How did you get there? Did you have a school uniform? Did your friends go to the same school? Which subjects were you good at and which were you bad at? Did you have a favourite teacher? Did you have school dinners? Did you move house? What did you think of the new town, neighbourhood? (Moving into puberty now.) How did your body change? Were you an early developer or a late developer? Did you have a boyfriend or a girlfriend? Were you in a gang? Did you have a nickname? Were you ever bullied? Did you do any bullying? Who was your best friend? Were you interested in fashion? Where did you have your hair done? Did you wear make-up, jewellery, a wristwatch, perfume? How much pocket money did you get? What did you spend it on? Did you go to church? Did you say prayers? Did you keep a diary? Did you write poetry? Did you go on a demonstration? Did you smoke a cigarette? Did you drink alcohol? Did you go to pubs, clubs, discos? Did you take recreational pharmaceuticals? Did you have homework? Did you do your homework? Did you take any exams? Did you win any prizes? Did you have your picture in the newspapers? Did you watch TV? Did you like comedy? Did you go to the theatre? Football matches? The opera? Glastonbury? Did you have a favourite band? Who was your favourite Beatle? Where did you go on holiday? How did you get on with your parents? Did you have birthday parties? Were you ill? Did you ever go to hospital? Did you go to a wedding or a funeral? Did you get into trouble with the police? Did you steal anything? Did you know anybody who was gay? Did you watch the news? Did you read a newspaper? How did you think you would vote in the election if you were old enough? What did you own? A computer, sound system, mobile phone, bicycle, iPod? How did you dress when you were going out for the evening when you were thirteen? (See yourself getting ready to go out aged thirteen.) At that age, what was the nature of your sexual experience? Did you know anyone who had died?

Characters Aged Thirteen to Fifteen

In Peter's story, this is the time that he moved to the new comprehensive school and met James, so the questions can explore this relationship.

Did you move house? Did you change school? What difference did these changes make? How did you get on at school? Who was your best friend? What subjects did you like and dislike? Did you have a

girlfriend or boyfriend? What did you do together?
Were you in love? Did you believe in God?
(Adolescence now.) How did your body change?
Were you embarrassed in the showers? Were you in a
team? Did you play any sports, games, or have any
hobbies? Did you win any prizes? How did you get
on with your parents? What did they look like? Did
you have a holiday job or a Saturday job? How much
money did you have? What did you spend it on? Did
you buy your own clothes? Did you have an 'image'?
Did you go to see bands? Did you collect anything?
Did you have a computer, a PlayStation? Did you
follow politics? Did you go on any demonstrations?
What did you like to read? Who was your favourite
author, playwright, comedian, filmmaker? Did you
listen to classical music? Did you watch football,
cricket, tennis? Did you write love letters? Did you
tweet? At age fifteen, what time did you have to be
home in the evening? Did you smoke? Drink? Take
drugs? Were you still a virgin at this age? How
sexually advanced were you? Did you have
homework? Revision? Extra tuition? Did you take any
exams? What did you own? Had you ever been on a
motorbike? What sort of car did the family have? Did
you go on holiday without your family? Did you go to
America? Were you given any careers advice? What
did you want to specialise in? Did you want to go to
university? Were you ill? Did you have any pregnancy
scares? Did you still have a nickname? Aged fifteen,
what did you think of your body? Which bits did you
like and which bits did you dislike? (Imagine yourself
in front of a mirror at the age of fifteen.)

Character Aged Fifteen to Eighteen

Did you move house? Did you change school? Did you
take any exams? Did you pass? What were your
grades? Did you do better or worse than expected?
Who were your girlfriends or boyfriends? Who was
your best friend? How did you get on with your
parents? Brothers and sisters? Did you go to church?

Were you in a sports team? Were you in a play? Were you in a band, choir, orchestra? Did you smoke, drink, take drugs? Did you go clubbing? Did you go to festivals? What did you want to do for a career? Did you belong to a 'tribe' – were you a Goth, a mod, an emo kid? How much money did you have? What did you spend it on? Did you owe money to anyone? Did you do your own washing? Did you go to restaurants? Where did you buy your clothes? Could you drive? Where did you go on holidays? Did your parents let your girlfriends or boyfriends sleep over? Did you go to a wedding? Did you go to the cinema? Did you register to vote? Did you read a newspaper? Did you watch the news? Did you know who the Foreign Secretary was? Did you get a holiday job? Did you want to go on to higher education? Did you go backpacking? Did you have a pregnancy scare? Did you join a political party? Did you get into a fight? What was your favourite film? Did you know anybody who had died? At the age of eighteen, locate your character in their bedroom, and in your imagination take them through the process of getting dressed to go on a date or an evening out. (Play the movie in your head…)

This is the time of Peter's relationship with Rachel and the events leading up to the play, so the questions should be tailored to incorporate detail of these events.

I also find that contemporary culture plays a large part in determining character. It is no longer the case, but it used to be possible to discover a great deal about the character simply by asking 'Who was your favourite Beatle?'

Working on the original production of *When You Cure Me*, we spent a considerable amount of time discussing the characters' record collections and the choices we made – Antony and the Johnsons, The Killers, Franz Ferdinand – became part of the soundtrack for the play. Recently I have initiated an exercise in which teenage characters set up their own Facebook accounts.

I use these exercises all the time, usually in the first week of rehearsals, and with groups of actors together. It helps them to focus on significant incidents in the background history of their characters. The questions vary from play to play, but the exercise always follows the education and home life of the characters in their formative years. It lays down the foundations of who they are going to be.

In addition, as with a devised piece, I work with each actor *individually* on creating his or her character's background story.

It is also important to keep checking the text to ensure that the character you are building is the person who ends up in the play. Actors often become proprietary and defensive about their characters and must be reminded that characters are brought into existence solely to serve the playwright's purpose. There's no point in getting to Act Three, Scene Seven, and having the Duke of Cornwall announce that his character would not blind Gloucester.

Shared Background Discussion

At the point in the chronology when Peter meets James, I brought the actor playing James into the rehearsal and we discussed the nature of their relationship in detail; similarly, when Peter meets Rachel and when James meets Alice. As in a devised play, actors are only allowed to have the information that their characters would have, so Rachel is not privy to discussions between James and Peter about her. The characters start to have their own secrets. We also played a game where we cast the other parts in the play: the characters who are mentioned but never seen; for example, Peter's mum. We decided on someone the actors all knew so that whenever she was mentioned the actors had the same image in their heads.

Research

Research is as important a component in building a character for a scripted play as it is in a devised piece. Research for *When You Cure Me* took the form of trips to Reading – to look at the school that the characters went to, to find the estate where they lived and the houses that they all lived in. We also found the shed where we thought Rachel could have been assaulted. We went to the mall they hung out in and went to The Purple Turtle, the club we imagined that the characters tried to get in to. We also looked at where they bought their clothes and tried some on in character. The actor playing Rachel had to research the symptoms of her condition and the police procedure she would have undergone after reporting the rape and assault.

Obviously, the research differs for every project and should always be regarded as a *part* of the process, not the *purpose* of the process. If your character has spent time in California, it is not entirely necessary to go there. California, like Reading, is a state of mind. The internet is perfect for this kind of research. I directed *Crooked*, a play by Catherine Trieschmann set in Oxford, Mississippi, and we were able to get detailed photographs of where everybody lived by Googling 'Oxford Mississippi Real Estate'.

A Little Less Conversation, A Little More Action

Let us say that we have now constructed life histories for all the characters, and the actors have shared information so everybody knows what they need to know about each other's stories. We have worked out and discussed the chronology of the various relationships. We know how many dates Peter and Rachel have been on, what happened and what they thought about it. We know the details of Peter's mother's illness and his involvement in her therapy. We know how many times James and Alice have split up and got back together again and the nature of their sexual relationship (explored using the hand exercise described earlier on page 12). We know the nature of Rachel's relationship with her mother and the details of her father's death, and we know what Rachel remembers about the attack and about the rape. We know the circumstances that lead up to the play. What we have are *biographies*. What we need now are *characters*.

Character is Biography in Action

Somewhat perversely, then, the process of getting into character starts with another visualisation exercise.

'A Day in the Life' Visualisation Exercise

What we do is to take the character through the events and scenes of one specific day in their lives. It is better to pick a day that has a fixed routine, say a day at work, and it is better at this stage to pick a day that is relatively trauma-free. Thus the actor playing Peter could concentrate on a day at school.

Having chosen the day, the time of year and the circumstances surrounding the character on this particular day, I again ask a series of questions, and the actor again plays the movie in his head.

> On this particular day, what time in the morning do you wake up? And how do you wake up? Alarm clock, radio, dawn chorus? If someone wakes you up, who are they, what do they look like, what do you talk about, and how do you feel about them? Is there anyone in bed with you? What are you wearing? Is it dark or is it light? Is it warm or is it cold? Take a look around the room you are sleeping in. How is it furnished? How is it

decorated? Where is the bed? Where are the windows?
Is there a wardrobe, chest of drawers, bedside table?
How is it lit? What else is in the room? Television, radio,
PlayStation, computer? (See the room in pictures, play
the movie in your head.)

And on this particular day, what time do you get out
of bed? How are you feeling? Are you warm, are you
cold? Are you ill, hungover, tired, excited? What are
you going to do on this particular day? In your own
time, go through the process of getting up. Do you
wash, shower, have a bath? Go on the journey to the
bathroom. What does the bathroom look like? Do you
meet anybody on the way? Who are they, what do
they look like, what do you talk about, how do you
feel about them? Do you wash your hair? Do you
shave? Do you put on make-up? Go through the
process of getting dressed on this particular day. How
much choice do you have about what to wear? How
long do you take to decide? Where do you get
dressed? Is anyone else there? (Play the movie in your
head…)

And where do you eat breakfast? Go through the
house. What do you eat? Who prepares it? Do you
enjoy it? Do you listen to the radio, watch television,
read a newspaper? Do you drink tea or coffee? Do
you have any post? Is there anyone else there? Are
you happy? What's the weather like? What do you
talk about?

Go on the first journey of the day. Where are you
going? How do you feel about it? When you leave the
house, what do you take with you? Overcoat,
umbrella, laptop, handbag, BlackBerry? What does
the house look like from outside? What does the
street look like? Is it sunny? Is it raining? Is it autumn,
summer?

Do you walk, go by car, take a bus? See the sights,
imagine the conversations on this particular day.

And what is your first destination of the day? Where
have you arrived? How do you feel about it? Go

through the events of the morning. What do you do? How do you feel about it? Do you go on any more journeys? Do you change your clothes? Who do you meet? What do you talk about?

Where do you go for lunch? What do you eat? Do you enjoy it? Do you go to a café, a canteen, a pub? Do you go home? How much do you spend? Do you have a drink? How are you feeling about the day so far?

What do you do on this particular afternoon? Where do you go? Who do you meet? What do you talk about? See all the locations. Imagine all the conversations on this particular afternoon.

What do you do in the evening? Do you go home? Do you change your clothes? Do you make any other journeys? Who do you meet? Do you watch TV? Do you surf the internet? Do you go to the pub, theatre, cinema? Do you play sports? Where do you have your evening meal?

What kind of day have you had? Are you happy? Are you in love? Are you angry? Are you jealous? Do you like yourself?

And what time do you go to bed on this particular day? In your own time, go through the process of getting ready for bed. (Play the movie in your head...) Is there anyone else there? What do you talk about? How do you feel about them? What time do you go to sleep? Do you dream?

As with all visualisation exercises, this is just a 'head' activity, and the questions can vary to suit the particular circumstances of the character and the play. Many actors have found this to be a useful warm-up and use it throughout the run of the show. I sometimes use a variation of this to unlock and examine emotionally sensitive events in the character's story. For example, when working on *When You Cure Me*, I constructed an exercise using the detail in the text of Rachel's description of the assault and rape to help the actor visualise the experience.

Interior Monologue

The next stage in the process is to give the actor an opportunity to take the biography and research, and use it to work out the physicality and rhythm of the character. For this I use a technique that has come to be known as 'interior monologue'. Again, I imagine that there are as many ways of approaching this as there are directors, but this is how it works for me.

In the rehearsal room we construct a simple set to represent a room in which the character spends time on their own. There's no need for complicated props or furniture, but chairs, tables, mattresses and rostra are useful. The actors construct their own environment to represent their imagined room. I always use hospital screens to define the area and to provide the actors with a limited and private space. The actor then chooses the day, the time of year and the circumstances in which the character finds him or herself alone in this room on this particular day. They need to know what their character has been doing and they need to know what they plan to do next. The actors repeat the 'day in the life' exercise until they arrive at the time when they are alone in the room, and they then try to inhabit the room as the character.

The objective now is to think as the character and then to vocalise those thoughts. This can be as simple as making a shopping list or thinking about the day ahead, or they can see where the character's fantasies take them. The actor playing Peter would probably again focus on the school day, thinking about the evening ahead when, say, he was going round to Rachel's house so they could revise together. His fantasies might include playing for the school football team, or something about Alice. Vocalising these thoughts does not mean that the characters talk to themselves; rather it provides an opportunity to experiment with the character's voice without the pressure of interaction in a scene. As they move around the room the actors should also begin to get a sense of the character's rhythm. Are they fast or slow? Heavy or light? Open or closed? In Laban Movement terms, this could be said to be the stage where we define the *efforts* of the characters, but from inside out rather than from outside in.

Actors are often tempted to invent imaginary telephones and telephone conversations while doing this exercise. This is a mistake, as the effort that goes into inventing both sides of an imaginary conversation gets in the way of concentrating on the interior monologue. Equally, the use of ornate props and extravagant mime is usually an unhelpful distraction.

Initially, actors will only be able to stay in character for short bursts, but this will lengthen as the exercise is repeated. It's a process of osmosis. With all this stuff, the golden rule is never to overcomplicate. Actors often try too hard; it's simply a matter of pretending to be somebody else. Kids do it all the time. (My daughter Flora was Pinocchio for months.)

At this point in rehearsals, we start to assemble rehearsal costumes, something for the actor to change into that changes *them*. It can be as simple as boots not shoes, a skirt not jeans, a shirt and tie, or a different aftershave. I used this exercise in character workshops at the Actors Centre, and Sheila Hancock once boldly announced that her character was wearing suspenders. The rehearsal costume should simply be whatever can be found that helps the actor to feel less like them and more like their character.

The next step is for the actors to take their characters for a walk. The simplest version of this is for the actor to walk a hundred yards in character or to wait for the bus. The purpose is to see the world through new eyes. Going shopping is also a useful trick: buy a newspaper or a bus ticket; decide where your character buys clothes and go there in character, try clothes on. It is important to get an idea of the character's fashion sense which, in turn, can also provide useful clues for the costume designer. The cast of *When You Cure Me* did this as part of their Reading research. Alice spent a lot of time in Miss Selfridge. It is important, however, to resist the temptation to buy anything expensive or that isn't needed. Despite constant warnings, one actor once bought an Armani suit and another bought an oil filter for a 1976 Ford Cortina. Although these character excursions are not strictly improvisations, they do nonetheless give actors an opportunity to think, walk and talk in character, outside the demands of the scene.

The purpose of all these exercises is to provide the iceberg of which the character in the play will be the tip. In the devising process, the next step would be to set up the improvisations that bring the characters together. But working on a script, the next step is to address the text and ask the second question:

Why Am I Saying This Stuff?

Text analysis can also take many forms. Stanislavsky adherents will use units and objectives. Others will 'action' every line, assigning a transitive verb to describe the intention or objective; the action one character adopts to affect another. As always, all these techniques are valid if they work for the actor, but whatever system you use the purpose remains the same: to find out the subtext – what is really going on between the lines. I should, however, emphasise that whatever system the actor or director uses, the character work must come before the text analysis in order to get coherent and useful results. It's impossible to make an informed decision about what the character might want without first decid-ing who they are.

When I devise a play, an important part of the process involves questioning the actors about the improvisation they have just participated in. If I have set up a scene in which two characters go out on a date, I will note what is said in the improvisation and then question the actors separately about what was happen-ing emotionally in the scene. One actor might say that when he described his interest in making plastic Airfix model aeroplanes, his date found this deeply fascinat-ing and that she was therefore clearly interested in entering into a steamy relationship with him. She, on the other hand, may say that she thought he was a complete tosspot and she had made it clear that she never wanted to see him again. It's where the stories don't match up that we find the play.

Discovering the subtext in a scripted play is a similar process.

The Read-through and Why to Avoid It

Before we start analysing the text, I think it's important to discuss the age-old ritual of the read-through. It is cus-tomary for the entire company of actors, writer, director, designer, lighting designer, sound designer, producer, general manager, literary manager and/or dramaturg, production manager, stage manager, CSM, DSM, ASM, marketing manager, development manager, box-office manager, finance manager, head of corporate affairs, press representative, health and safety officer, cultural diversity monitor and all their various assistants to meet up on the first morning of rehearsals for a cup of tea and a muffin. This is so everybody can meet everyone con-nected with the production for what is probably the last time before the press-night party; so it's probably the only time they will ever meet sober. This is all very useful and to be encouraged. In America the 'meet and greet' can go on for days, as there are legions of extra execs and interns performing functions not yet invented in British theatre, and there are infinitely more varieties of muffin. In Japan there is a considerable amount of bowing.

What happens is that the producer makes a speech of welcome and tells everyone why they can't have any comps, and everyone shuffles about muttering nervously for half an hour and nobody touches the food. The theatre staff cling together shyly in one corner, while the actors try to remember when they last worked together on *Holby City*, and the techies are either discussing the price of Artex or are outside having a smoke. Eventually, the designer shows everybody the model of the set, explaining how they arrived at their exciting concept... and then the actors sit at a table in a gloomy circle and read the play. This can go either way. Sometimes the play sings, the actors are wonderful, talented, beautiful and witty, and the assembled execs and others return to their perches convinced that we will all be in the Wyndham's by lunchtime. More often, what you get is nervy, indifferent and frequently inaudible, and everyone loses the will to live. Either way, the director is left to pick up the pieces. This is not entirely an exaggeration.

I am not in any way suggesting here that actors are such nervous and precious creatures that they will be in some way damaged by reading the play out loud in a room full of strangers. That's pretty much why they joined. The problem is more with the temptation to perform and come up with instant character and interpretative decisions before anyone has had time to work on the play. If an actor gets a laugh or a big reaction during the read-through, they may well persuade themselves that they have solved the line – and you, as the director, are stuck with this version in perpetuity. The corollary of this is that not all actors are good at instant readings, and it is possible for playwrights and/or producers to convince themselves that they have made a casting mistake. A Very Famous Playwright once told me how he and a Very Famous Director were once so convinced of this after a readthrough of one of his plays that they had the Very Famous Actor replaced. Very Famous Playwright subsequently realised that he had made a big mistake. Although this is an extreme example, I have often known writers and producers trying to dink about with a play on the strength of the first morning's ritual exposure, and to no real purpose. If you expect the finished product on day one, there seems little point in anyone turning up again before the tech.

The point is: you can't tell anything from a readthrough, not even how long the play is.

I prefer to get rid of everybody before the actors read the play out loud, and even then give clear instructions about keeping it simple and avoiding the urge to be impressive. Quite often I will swap round the parts. This prevents anyone from acquiring bad habits from the start or resorting to phoney histrionics for effect.

There has also recently been an outbreak, among certain actors and directors, of the belief that it may be in some way beneficial for actors to have learnt their lines *before* rehearsals begin. This may be appropriate in film or television where it's a miracle if there are any rehearsals at all, and was possibly relevant in the days of weekly rep, but seems to me patently ludicrous – especially when applied to productions at our major subsidised houses where rehearsal periods often extend for months. How can you possibly learn a line before you have worked out who you are and why you say it? The process of discovering the answers to these questions is the purpose of rehearsal, and it has to be a collective and collaborative process – onanistic process results in onanistic performance.

If we have successfully avoided the ritual of the read-through, we will have consulted and referenced the text throughout the character-building process. This is the point in rehearsal where we use that information to take us into the subtext, and we begin to read the play with informed insight.

When You Cure Me: Act One, Scene One

At the beginning of the rehearsal process, the actors should make notes on what happens in the play from their character's point of view. For example, this is Peter's version of what happens to him in Scene One, in terms of physical action:

> January 17th: Peter visits Rachel for the first time since she was raped and assaulted. She is asleep in bed. She stirs in her sleep. Peter talks softly to her and she wakes up. Peter asks her if she has had a bad dream. Rachel takes his hand. Peter tries to take it away, but doesn't know how. Rachel says she needs to pee. Peter suggests calling her mum but Rachel wants Peter to help her. Peter agrees and finds the bedpan under the bed. He helps Rachel onto it. He is rather rough. Rachel asks Peter to remove her knickers. Peter does so, being careful not to look. He holds her pants in his hand and then purposefully puts them in his pocket. Rachel asks Peter if he would prefer to call her mother, but Peter stoically declines and continues to help Rachel onto the bedpan. He has to support her while she pees. Rachel asks him to hold on to her tightly to help her balance. She doesn't want her mother sniffing around. After a long moment Rachel starts to pee. Peter hears her. He gets Rachel some toilet paper. She wipes herself, depositing the tissue in the bedpan. Rachel tells Peter to empty the

bedpan in the bathroom and not to look 'as there will be blood'. Peter leaves Rachel alone as he goes to the bathroom, where he checks out the bedpan before returning to Rachel.

Silence.

Then Peter reports that there wasn't much blood – he thought she would like to know. Rachel asks for her knickers back. Peter takes them from his pocket and helps Rachel to put them back on. Peter says that he will buy Rachel some Baby Wipes so she can clean her hands when she 'goes to the loo'. Peter encourages Rachel to tell him when she wants him to go. Rachel says that she is pleased that he is here. Peter has spoken to James, who has asked after her. James has got back together with Alice. Alice has said some nice things. Rachel is disinterested. Peter uses his asthma inhaler. Peter tells Rachel that everyone at school is being nice about it all. Rachel explains that her paralysis is psychological and that her legs will heal soon – the doctors have 'basically promised'. Peter tries to understand all this.

Rachel asks Peter to help her to sit up in bed. He tries, but she screams in pain. She asks him to try again. He refuses because it hurts her. She insists, and eventually and painfully Peter manoeuvres Rachel into a sitting position. The effort causes Peter to take another toke on his inhaler. Rachel says that she feels older. Peter doesn't. Rachel asks Peter to get into bed with her. Peter worries that this will cause Rachel more discomfort, but Rachel insists and Peter gets in, clinging to the edge of the bed so Rachel has to pull him in closer. Rachel says it's nice. She can feel Peter's heartbeat. He is nervous. Rachel asks if her scar bothers Peter. He says it doesn't, that he still thinks she's pretty. Rachel enjoys the closeness. Peter tells Rachel that Mr Norris has asked if she would like him to set her some work and that Mr Edwards suggested that Peter talk to him about 'it' and that

Peter should call him Geoff. Rachel snuggles up to Peter. She enjoys the closeness and then discovers that he has a stiffy. Peter denies this and tries to pull himself away. He apologises and then apologises some more. Rachel is upset and confused. Peter is upset and confused. She asks Peter to hold her but then tells him to get out of the bed. Peter tries to explain but fails. He tries to hide his erection, uses his inhaler and apologises again. He doesn't know what to do, so continues to apologise.

Blackout.

So that's what happens in the scene. Now we have to find out what's really going on behind the physical action.

What I do now is sit around a table with the actors and the writer, and forensically analyse the text. This includes elements of both actioning and identifying objectives, but allows for the character to exhibit a certain amount of contradictory motivation. We begin by determining the character's state of mind as the play opens:

Peter has not seen or spoken to Rachel since she was attacked. He knows she was raped. He knows she was cut with a knife and he knows that she is now paralysed from the waist down. He knows that she has not been able to speak about the incident. He doesn't know what to do and he doesn't know what to expect. Back at school he has become the focus of attention and sympathy, particularly from Alice. The power has shifted in his relationship with James. He wonders how Rachel will have changed. He's aware that she's no longer a virgin. He wants to help. He has absolutely no idea what to do. He goes to visit Rachel.

Below is a possible version of Peter's subtext in Scene One.

Text	Peter's Subtext
	I don't know what to do.
	Why am I here?
PETER (*soft, so soft*). You awake…	
She's not awake, she's just sort of stretching her mouth, so he sits back. This takes for ever.	
	She's moving. Is she okay?
She moves again.	
	Is she having a bad dream?
	Should I wake her up?
Rach…	
Pause.	
	Or shouldn't I?
	Should I go?
	No, I'll stay.
Rach…	
Pause.	
	I will be tough.
(*Louder.*) Rachel…	
Pause.	
	Try harder.
Rachel, you awake…	
	I'll touch her arm.
	Was that a mistake?
RACHEL. Wha…	
PETER (*reaching out and touching her arm again, his hand rests on the side of the bed*). Hi.	
	I am going to be as nice and loving and caring as possible.
Pause.	
	Please wake up so I don't have to go on with this.
Rachel?	
RACHEL. Uh… Di' you?	

She retches like she's about to throw up, but stops herself.

Pause.

PETER. Bad dream, or…

How are you? Are you in pain?

I am trying to be really calm but I don't know what to do.

RACHEL (*takes his hand in hers*). No.

Pause. He tries to take his hand away, but he doesn't know how.

This is embarrassing. I'll pretend it isn't.

I need to pee…

Help! What do I do?

PETER. Okay.

I'll pretend to be confident.

RACHEL. I, uh…

Please let me call your mum.

She'll know what to do.

PETER. Shall I call your mum or…

Please let me call your mum.

I don't know what to do.

RACHEL. No. Don't call her.

Oh! Shit!

PETER. Okay. Are you…

I can cope with this, I think.

What happens now?

RACHEL. Can you do it?

Oh! Shit!

PETER. Really? Sure.

> **I'd help if I could but I'm
> embarrassed.**
>
> **What do I do?**

RACHEL. There's a pan under the bed.

PETER. Okay.

> **I am going to appear to be
> efficient, caring and
> confident.**

*He grasps under the bed, which is pretty cluttered,
for the bedpan.*

> **I am completely in control.**

(*Desperately casual.*) What does it look like?

RACHEL. Blue.

PETER. Yeah.

> **I knew that.**

He re-emerges with it.

RACHEL. There should be a, there's a insert under there
too – just cardboard – there's a stack of them – they
just slot in – the insert should…

He finds the cardboard insert.

PETER. Is this…

> **I'm getting the hang of
> this.**

RACHEL. Yeah. Pass it here, it sort of clips in.

PETER. No. I can do it…

> **I can cope. I am being very
> grown up and you should
> be impressed.**

*He inserts it clumsily and then he goes to the end of
the bed and lifts her legs, quite roughly. He's
improvising and being slightly rough with it, so that
when he attempts to slide the bedpan underneath,
she immediately falls off.*

RACHEL (*warning*). Peter…

> **I am doing great.**

PETER. Am I… What?

          **Oh God. Am I doing this
wrong?**

          I'm really trying.

RACHEL. You're being rough... a bit...

          Shit! Shit! Shit!

PETER. Oh...

          I'm mortified.

Beat.

          What do I do now?

RACHEL. Um. My knickers...

          **Oh no. She wants me to
take off her knickers. I
want to be helpful and
caring and I don't want her
to think it's sexual. It's not.
Promise.**

PETER. Yeah.

*He does so gently, and blindly, sliding them off her
by the knicker-straps, and being careful not to look.
Then he holds the knickers, unsure of what to do
with them.*

          That went well.

RACHEL. Do you want to... get Mum...

PETER (*puts the knickers in his pocket with confidence*).
It's okay.

          No, I can cope, honestly.

*He hesitates and then gently lifts her legs and slides
the bedpan on.*

RACHEL. You have to keep hold of me, so I don't – Sorry,
I don't want to slip off.

PETER. No. No. It's fine.

          **This is really difficult. I
want her to be impressed.**

RACHEL. I just don't want Mum sniffing...

          Sniffing? Oh, I see.

PETER. It's fine. I'm pleased.

I'm doing really well.

He holds her by the hips, trying to keep this as non-sexual as possible.

Pause. She hasn't started peeing yet, she's sweating slightly, this is very difficult.

Okay?

I'm good at being caring.

RACHEL. Yeah.

Pause.

This is agony.

I'm slipping, grip tighter…

PETER. Like this.

Please can this be over.

RACHEL. Yeah.

**I wish this wasn't
happening.**

PETER *tightens and doesn't know which way to look, so he just looks at her, and she stares at him and they're stuck like this and it's perfect and horrible. Then, finally, she starts to pee. It's hard for her to pee, and she only gives up a pathetic amount, but it seems to make a huge clattering noise as it dribbles into the cardboard bedpan. PETER doesn't breathe until she finishes.*

You need to get me the toilet tissue.

That wasn't so bad.

PETER. Is that…? Are you balanced?

This is going well.

RACHEL (*moves her own hands in order to steady herself*). Yeah.

He gently lets go, leaving her balancing on the bedpan whilst he finds the toilet paper. He finds it.

PETER. Do you…

**Please don't make me wipe
your bum.**

RACHEL. Yeah. Give it here.

Phew!

He hands her the toilet roll, she wipes herself whilst looking precariously balanced. He moves as if to help at one point, but holds back. She deposits the tissue in the bedpan.

You empty it in the toilet – and there's a bin in there – for the, uh, insert.

PETER. Okay…

> **Right. I am going to be really efficient now.**

He reaches in again, helps her balance herself, and then slides her off the bedpan.

RACHEL. Don't look at it – there'll be blood…

> **I can deal with this and show her how caring and loving I am.**

PETER. Okay.

He takes the bedpan out of the room, carefully averting his eyes. We're left with just her. She shifts on the bed and winces. She touches the scar on her cheek, she traces it with her fingers. She tries to shift up on the bed, but she winces again and gags, this really hurts.

(Re-entering.) Okay…

> **See how well I handled all that and I checked for blood.**
>
> **I think this could be a little more hygienic.**

RACHEL. Yeah.

PETER *sits by her bed. They sit in silence, then she takes his hand.*

PETER. There wasn't much blood.

> **I'm a helpful grown-up.**

RACHEL. Wasn't there?

> **I thought that was impressive.**

PETER. I thought you'd want to know – there wasn't…

> **I'm being solicitous.**

Beat. She watches him.

> **What have I done wrong?**

RACHEL. You need to give me my knickers back…

PETER (*laughs through his nose*). Yeah. Um…

> **Shit, how embarrassing.**

He finds the knickers in his pocket and starts putting them on her legs. He's rough again, like he was with the first attempt at the bedpan. She waits until he finishes and then moves her own hands down to straighten up his attempts.

They sit in silence for a moment.

> **I am going to give some generous advice now.**

I could get you some of those Baby Wipes. For your hands, so that when you go to the loo, you can clean them too. Because you don't want them dirty – I thought –

RACHEL. Okay.

> **This is a good plan. This is going well.**

PETER. I'll get them tonight. When I leave… or…

RACHEL. Yeah. Okay.

PETER. Just say when you've had enough basically…

> **Tell me you want me to stay.**

Pause.

> **Go on.**

RACHEL. I'm really pleased… you're here.

> **Great.**

PETER. Yeah? I spoke to James last night…

> **I know you don't like James.**

RACHEL. Okay.

> **No, he really likes you.**

PETER. He asked after you. He sounded worried.

He does.

RACHEL (*non-committal*). Okay.

Really.

PETER. They've got back together, him and Alice. He
sounded really pleased about it, she said some really
nice stuff to him too, about it all…

**Alice has been really great
to me.**

**I don't fancy her but she's
nice actually.**

RACHEL. Okay.

This is really hard.

They sit in silence again. PETER *takes a Ventolin
asthma inhaler from his trousers and takes a squirt.*

PETER. Everyone's being really nice about it… you. I
mean, everyone's saying nice things…

Please talk to me.

RACHEL (*soft*). There's no reason, for the legs – it's just
me –

PETER. Yeah?

**I really want to
understand.**

RACHEL. It'll go away –

You don't have to tell me.

PETER. Okay.

**I don't understand what's
happened.**

RACHEL. They think it'll go away soon – sometimes it
just does – they basically promised. Will you help
me sit up…

How do I do this?

PETER. Yeah. You just want another cushion behind you
or…

RACHEL. No. Just sitting up…

This should be fine.

PETER. Okay.

He leans over her, and holds her by her armpits. He starts to haul her up the bed, so she's higher on the headboard. But then she screams and he stops. He doesn't speak, he just makes a noise.

Pause.

Oh my God! What have I done?

RACHEL (*getting her breath back*). It's fine.

Pause.

This is awful.

PETER. I didn't –

Sorry, sorry, sorry.

RACHEL. It's fine.

Sorry, sorry, sorry.

Pause. They both get their breath back.

Pull me up a bit higher, would you?

No.

PETER. What? No! It hurts you.

Don't make me.

RACHEL. I want to be up higher.

I don't want to hurt you.

PETER. No, I…

Please don't make me do it.

RACHEL. Please, Peter.

PETER. Why?

Why make me hurt you?

RACHEL. Can you help me, please?

I don't want to but I will for you.

He gingerly fingers his arms around her armpits and attempts to pull her higher on the headboard. He starts carefully, but he has to tug her up, so he can't be gentle. She gags slightly at the effort, but manages to stop herself from screaming.

(*Again waiting a moment for breath.*) Thank you.

126

This is dreadful.

They sit a moment longer. PETER *is white-faced. He pulls out and takes another tug from his inhaler.*

PETER. Are you okay?

I warned you it would hurt.

RACHEL. I feel older, do you know that?

What do you mean?

PETER. Yeah? I don't particularly. Is that –

Am I supposed to? Is it a symptom?

Beat.

Have I said something wrong?

RACHEL. Will you get in with me?

What does she want? Is this about sex? Help.

PETER. Yeah?

Are you sure? What do you want?

RACHEL. Will you…

I'm not sure about this.

PETER. It won't hurt?

RACHEL. No.

What shall I do?

Beat.

Is this what she really wants or is she doing it for me?

PETER. That wasn't what that was about, was it? Getting up higher.

Please don't do this on my behalf.

RACHEL. No.

PETER. You weren't making it so I could get in. Moving up, so…

> **Are you sure about this?**

RACHEL. Will you get in?

> **I don't want to do this.**

PETER. Yeah.

He squeezes himself onto the bed, so that his hips are just on the side of the bed. She pulls him in closer, and partly curls what parts of the body she can around him.

Can you, uh –

> **Oh God, I nearly asked her to move over.**

RACHEL. This is nice.

PETER. Yeah.

> **This is terrifying. Please don't let me get a stiffy.**

RACHEL. I can feel your heartbeat, it's going quick actually…

PETER. Is it?

> **Oh no. I must stay cool.**

RACHEL. Yeah. (*Takes his hand and puts it on his heart.*)

PETER. Yeah.

> **This is nice but scary.**

RACHEL. You're nervous, that's all –

> **No shit, Sherlock!**

Beat.

> **What do I do now?**

(*Soft.*) Do you mind the scar?

PETER. No.

> **Of course I don't mind the scar but I don't know if I love you.**

RACHEL. It'll fade. I mean, I'll look the same…

> **I must reassure her.**

PETER. You're really pretty. You still are.

> **I do still fancy her.**

Beat.

Relax, relax, relax.

RACHEL. This is nice. I like it like this.

She feels her hand around and sort of pats him.

PETER (*giggle*). Oh. Um. Mr Norris asked if you wanted work set, by the way.

She giggles.

And Mr Edwards, though he was weird about it, he said I had to talk to him, well, if I wanted to, and that I had to call him Geoff…

RACHEL (*giggle*). Geoff!

This is fun.

PETER (*giggle*). Yeah.

Pause. She tries to snuggle up.

Stay cool.

RACHEL. I'm really happy just like this…

PETER. Yeah.

RACHEL. Geoff!

PETER (*giggle*). Yeah.

I'm enjoying this.

RACHEL. What did you do?

I'll make her laugh.

PETER. I don't know. Ran away.

She smiles. Pause, a long luxury pause. They breathe into each other.

Oh no. I'm getting a stiffy.

RACHEL. I wish we could just stay like this…

PETER. Yeah.

Please don't notice.

Pause.

Please don't notice.

RACHEL (*suddenly whitens*). Peter. Is that… Peter? Have you got an erection?

It's not what you think.

PETER. No.

He shifts his groin backwards.

                         Make it go away.

RACHEL. Yes. Ow.

PETER. No.

                         It's not because I want a shag.

RACHEL. Peter – you can't – ow –

PETER. I can't – I'm sorry –

                         I can't make it go away.

He moves his arms back, he tries to find space, he can't. She growls like a cat, pure frustration. He's almost in tears.

                         I'm mortified. I don't want to rape you.

Sorry – I can't…

                         I can't move.

RACHEL. I can *feel* it – uh – uh –

He's trying to pull everything away from her.

PETER. Don't, don't, I'm sorry. I'm sorry.

                         Don't be upset.

                         It's not about sex.

Beat.

I'm sorry.

                         I hate myself.

Beat. He's as far back as he can be, yet he still flurries some more, trying to find more space.

I'm so sorry. Rachel… Rachel…

                         Please forgive me.

RACHEL (*half-spoken*). Okay.

Beat. She's struggling to control her tears. He concentrates on holding his stomach in.

PETER. Sorry –

                         I hate myself.

RACHEL. No.

                         It won't go down.

PETER. Sorry, shall I get off –

Beat.

Please let me get off the bed.

RACHEL. Hold me.

PETER. Sorry. I'm so sorry.

Please forgive me.

Pause. She moves towards him. He tries to evade as much of her as possible, but she's more aggressive than he is.

Pause.

RACHEL. No. Get off.

PETER. Sorry. I'm really…

Thank God.

He half-falls off the bed in relief.

I wasn't trying to shag you now you are no longer a virgin. I wasn't aroused on purpose.

It's not. It doesn't mean I expect… it's not like a signal or…

Beat. She can't speak. He tries to stand in a way that minimises the erection. He takes another squirt from his inhaler, he's in a panic.

I'm really really sorry, I just don't know what to do… That's all. Sorry.

Beat.

Please make this stop.

RACHEL (*swallow*). Okay.

I want to go. I can't do this.

PETER. I feel sick. I'm really sorry.

Pause. PETER can't decide whether to leave or not. He's determined not to look at the door until he does.

(*Soft, his mouth doesn't work properly.*) I'm not sure what I'm supposed to do…

Pause. He straightens his back, the erection has finally subsided.

> **Don't hate me.**

Rachel…

Pause.

> **I don't know what to do.**

Rach…

RACHEL (*looks up finally, meets his face*). Yeah?

> **Please make everything all right.**

PETER. Sorry? Sorry.

Blackout.

So that's a version of Peter's subtext in Act One, Scene One. Rachel's subtext is obviously a different matter. Text is what characters say. Subtext is what characters mean.

We now work through the entire play uncovering the subtext. It's also important to find out what happens between the scenes. For example, we need to know what Peter is telling James and Alice about the situation, and what information and attitude every character brings into every scene. How does Alice's attitude towards Peter change her relationship with James? Later in the play, Peter disappears for several days. The actor playing Peter needs to work out where he went and what he did.

So having asked 'Who am I?' and 'Why am I saying this stuff?', we need to ask the third question:

Where Do I Sit?

I have never been able to do blocking. I can organise complicated scene-changes in an interesting way and marshal crowds and objects around the stage in an attractive fashion. I can even turn my hand to choreographing a dance routine and an occasional outbreak of performance art, but I can't do blocking. I don't know how it works. I just don't understand how it is possible to sit down with a script and, before rehearsals, work out on which particular line a character will want to sit on the sofa or cross to the French windows, unless of course they have a line about being able to see Marlow on a clear day. There is nothing, in my opinion, more counter-productive than forcing actors to stagger about the stage with scripts in their hands and, without character or purpose, trying to remember where to sit.

A friend of mine was once in a production of *Lady Audley's Secret*, directed by a Famous Dame of the Theatre. After a jolly muffin and a counterproductive read-through, the Famous Dame started to block the play. By the middle of the afternoon's rehearsal, they had got halfway through Act Three and all was confusion. Eventually, a young actor spoke up: 'I'm sorry, but can we stop? It's just that I'm afraid I have no idea where my character is coming from in this scene.' Without looking up, the Famous Dame consulted her heavily annotated prompt copy. 'Up-right, darling. Now shall we carry on from when you pick up the tea tray?'

Where characters need to be onstage is dependent on the psychological circumstances of the scene, and is dictated by the body language between them. This cannot be investigated unless we first know *who they are*, *what they are doing* and *why*. And in that order.

It's Off to Work We Go

So how do we get the play on its feet? There is a useful exercise I use all the time that evolved out of solving a particular problem. Several years ago, I was directing a play at the Bush called *Dead Sheep* by Catherine Johnson. The play told the story of three female recovering alcoholics on an outward-bound trek up the Brecon Beacons with a born-again Christian dwarf and a psychotic ex-soldier. The late great Katrin Cartlidge gave a stunning performance as a silent and traumatised Goth. The play opens with the three women and the dwarf unpacking their kit, pitching two tents and cooking potatoes on a Primus stove. There was also non-stop dialogue. The choreography was very complicated and had to be timed to the lines, so, after working on character and subtext, I hit on the idea of reading out all the lines of the scene myself while the actors (in character but without having to speak) concentrated on the tenting caper. After repeating the exercise several times we found we had evolved a route map for the physical activity in the scene, while making it work organically in terms of character, subtext and fitting the lines into the action.

So, what I do now is read the text out loud and, where necessary, the stage directions, as the actors move through the scene discovering where they need to go. It's a very simple and very effective way of getting the play on its feet without actually blocking it. Nobody ever believes that this works until they try it. What we end up with is a physical version of the play which continually evolves as we rehearse.

It may seem unnecessary in a play like *When You Cure Me,* in which the central character never leaves her bed and the others circle around her, but the decisions that the actors make about their character's proximity to Rachel and to each other as the tale is told are an important dimension in the dynamic of the play. Obviously, as a director it's my job to make sure that all this is successfully illuminating the story to the audience. If the actor playing Peter were to suggest that he spent the entire first act hiding in Rachel's wardrobe because his character had been traumatised by the sudden departure of his father, the director's correct response should be: 'Don't be a twat all your life, Timothy. Have a day off.'

Directing is Ninety Per Cent Buddhism and Ten Per Cent Fascism

So having answered the 'three big questions' we can now begin to discover the shape and rhythm of the play and work on how we tell the tale to the audience. The character and subtext work is to provide a solid platform from which the actors and the play can take off. They have to trust that the groundwork will support them as they stop playing the rehearsals and start playing the play. It's like working out the notes and the chords so that when the show hits an audience they can play jazz. It may sound perverse, but the reason for doing all this preparation is precisely so that when the actors get on stage they can forget it and just play in the moment.

To make it work you have to trust the actors and they have to trust you. It's hard work and they have to be prepared to commit to the whole excursion. It won't work with actors who only want to read the brochure.

Of course, there are many people working in theatre today who think this is all a pile of dreadful old toss and an unnecessary self-indulgence.

David Mamet in his overheated pamphlet *True and False – Heresy and Common Sense for the Actor* even went as far as to suggest that there is no such thing as character. He must have forgotten to tell Pacino. Equally, devotees of Post-dramatic Theatre argue that plot, character and dramatic structure are now an irrelevance. I remain unconvinced.

It seems to me that the essential bargain of theatre is that a group of human beings get together with another group of human beings, and collectively they try to find ways to enrich the experience of being human. In my experience, I think that working through truth and character is the best way to make this happen. I also believe in having fun.

WHEN YOU CURE ME
by Jack Thorne

For Chris Thorne and Fiona Bleach

When You Cure Me was first performed at the Bush Theatre, London, on 16 November 2005, with the following cast:

PETER	Samuel Barnett
RACHEL	Morven Christie
JAMES	Daniel Bayle
ALICE	Lisa McDonald
ANGELA	Gwyneth Strong
Director	Mike Bradwell
Designer	Penelope Challen
Lighting Designer	Tanya Burns
Sound Designer	Nick Manning

When You Cure Me received its first workshops as part of the National Youth Theatre's Short Nyts season in August 2004, directed by Vicky Jones. The play was subsequently commissioned by the Bush Theatre.

Characters

PETER, *seventeen*
RACHEL, *seventeen*
JAMES, *seventeen*
ALICE, *seventeen*
ANGELA, *forty-two*

Set

A teenage girl's bedroom. The play takes place in Reading over a period of three months, from January to March.

Rachel's Injuries

Rachel has a long inflamed scar down the side of her face. Surrounding the scar is severe bruising that puffs her eye. The cut gets less inflamed as the play progresses and by Act Four there's no bruising at all, just the scar. Stiffness in the rest of her body also gradually dissipates. In particular, in Act One she has trouble with her left hand and wrist but by Act Three she's moving it as if normal. But the main damage sustained is that Rachel can't move her legs, and has very little movement in the base to the middle of her spine. She is bedbound and moving her body is very painful because the rest of her spine is forced to take a weight and pressure it's not used to, but she does have some movement and some control of her bowels.

ACT ONE

1.1

17th January.

In the blackout.

PETER (*soft, so soft*). You awake…

> *The lights rise gently. She's not awake, she's just sort of stretching her mouth, so he sits back. This takes for ever.*
>
> *She moves again.*
>
> Rach…
>
> *Pause.*
>
> Rach…
>
> *Pause.*
>
> (*Louder.*) Rachel…
>
> *Pause. The lights are at full brightness.*
>
> Rachel, you awake…

RACHEL. Wha…

PETER (*reaching out and touching her arm again, his hand rests on the side of the bed*). Hi.

> *Pause.*
>
> Rachel?

RACHEL. Uh… Di' you?

> *She retches like she's about to throw up, but stops herself.*
>
> *Pause.*

PETER. Bad dream, or…

RACHEL (*takes his hand in hers*). No.

> *Pause. He tries to take his hand away, but he doesn't know how.*
>
> I need to pee…

PETER. Okay.

RACHEL. I, uh…

PETER. Shall I call your mum or…

RACHEL. No. Don't call her.

PETER. Okay. Are you…

RACHEL. Can you do it?

PETER. Really? Sure.

RACHEL. There's a pan under the bed.

PETER. Okay.

He grasps under the bed, which is pretty cluttered, for the bedpan.

(*Desperately casual.*) What does it look like?

RACHEL. Blue.

PETER. Yeah.

He re-emerges with it.

RACHEL. There should be a, there's a insert under there too –
just cardboard – there's a stack of them – they just slot in –
the insert should…

He finds the cardboard insert.

PETER. Is this…

RACHEL. Yeah. Pass it here, it sort of clips in.

PETER. No. I can do it…

He inserts it clumsily and then he goes to the end of the bed and lifts her legs, quite roughly. He's improvising and being slightly rough with it, so that when he attempts to slide the bedpan underneath, she immediately falls off.

RACHEL (*warning*). Peter…

PETER. Am I… What?

RACHEL. You're being rough… a bit…

PETER. Oh…

Beat.

RACHEL. Um. My knickers…

PETER. Yeah.

He does so gently, and blindly, sliding them off her by the knicker-straps, and being careful not to look. Then he holds the knickers, unsure of what to do with them.

RACHEL. Do you want to… get Mum…

PETER (*puts the knickers in his pocket with confidence*). It's okay.

He hesitates and then gently lifts her legs and slides the bedpan on.

RACHEL. You have to keep hold of me, so I don't – Sorry, I don't want to slip off.

PETER. No. No. It's fine.

RACHEL. I just don't want Mum sniffing…

PETER. It's fine. I'm pleased.

He holds her by the hips, trying to keep this as non-sexual as possible. From the floor below we faintly hear the sound of The Archers *theme music kicking off.*

Pause. She hasn't started peeing yet, she's sweating slightly, this is very difficult.

Okay?

RACHEL. Yeah.

Pause.

I'm slipping, grip tighter…

PETER. Like this.

RACHEL. Yeah.

PETER *tightens and doesn't know which way to look, so he just looks at her, and she stares at him and they're stuck like this and it's perfect and horrible. Then, finally, she starts to pee. It's hard for her to pee, and she only gives up a pathetic amount, but it seems to make a huge clattering noise as it dribbles into the cardboard bedpan.* PETER *doesn't breathe until she finishes.*

You need to get me the toilet tissue.

PETER. Is that…? Are you balanced?

RACHEL (*moves her own hands in order to steady herself*). Yeah.

He gently lets go, leaving her balancing on the bedpan whilst he finds the toilet paper. He finds it.

PETER. Do you…

RACHEL. Yeah. Give it here.

He hands her the toilet roll, she wipes herself whilst looking precariously balanced. He moves as if to help at one point, but holds back. She deposits the tissue in the bedpan.

You empty it in the toilet – and there's a bin in there – for the, uh, insert.

PETER. Okay…

He reaches in again, helps her balance herself, and then slides her off the bedpan.

RACHEL. Don't look at it – there'll be blood…

PETER. Okay.

He takes the bedpan out of the room, carefully averting his eyes. We're left with just her. She shifts on the bed and winces. She touches the scar on her cheek, she traces it with her fingers. She tries to shift up on the bed, but she winces again and gags, this really hurts.

(Re-entering.) Okay…

RACHEL. Yeah.

PETER *sits by her bed. They sit in silence, then she takes his hand.*

PETER. There wasn't much blood.

RACHEL. Wasn't there?

PETER. I thought you'd want to know – there wasn't…

Beat. She watches him.

RACHEL. You need to give me my knickers back…

PETER *(laughs through his nose)*. Yeah. Um…

He finds the knickers in his pocket and starts putting them on her legs. He's rough again, like he was with the first attempt at the bedpan. She waits until he finishes and then moves her own hands down to straighten up his attempts.

They sit in silence for a moment.

I could get you some of those Baby Wipes. For your hands, so that when you go to the loo, you can clean them too. Because you don't want them dirty – I thought –

RACHEL. Okay.

PETER. I'll get them tonight. When I leave… or…

RACHEL. Yeah. Okay.

PETER. Just say when you've had enough basically…

Pause.

RACHEL. I'm really pleased… you're here.

PETER. Yeah? I spoke to James last night…

RACHEL. Okay.

PETER. He asked after you. He sounded worried.

RACHEL (*non-committal*). Okay.

PETER. They've got back together, him and Alice. He sounded really pleased about it, she said some really nice stuff to him too, about it all…

RACHEL. Okay.

They sit in silence again. PETER *takes a Ventolin asthma inhaler from his trousers and takes a squirt.*

PETER. Everyone's being really nice about it… you. I mean, everyone's saying nice things…

RACHEL (*soft*). There's no reason, for the legs – it's just me –

PETER. Yeah?

RACHEL. It'll go away –

PETER. Okay.

RACHEL. They think it'll go away soon – sometimes it just does – they basically promised. Will you help me sit up…

PETER. Yeah. You just want another cushion behind you or…

RACHEL. No. Just sitting up…

PETER. Okay.

He leans over her, and holds her by her armpits. He starts to haul her up the bed, so she's higher on the headboard. But then she screams and he stops. He doesn't speak, he just makes a noise.

Pause.

RACHEL (*getting her breath back*). It's fine.

Pause.

PETER. I didn't –

RACHEL. It's fine.

Pause. They both get their breath back.

Pull me up a bit higher, would you?

PETER. What? No! It hurts you.

RACHEL. I want to be up higher.

PETER. No, I…

RACHEL. Please, Peter.

PETER. Why?

RACHEL. Can you help me, please?

He gingerly fingers his arms around her armpits and attempts to pull her higher on the headboard. He starts carefully, but he has to tug her up, so he can't be gentle. She gags slightly at the effort, but manages to stop herself from screaming.

(Again waiting a moment for breath.) Thank you.

They sit a moment longer. PETER is white-faced. He pulls out and takes another tug from his inhaler.

PETER. Are you okay?

RACHEL. I feel older, do you know that?

PETER. Yeah? I don't particularly. Is that –

Beat.

RACHEL. Will you get in with me?

PETER. Yeah?

RACHEL. Will you…

PETER. It won't hurt?

RACHEL. No.

Beat.

PETER. That wasn't what that was about, was it? Getting up higher.

RACHEL. No.

PETER. You weren't making it so I could get in. Moving up, so…

RACHEL. Will you get in?

PETER. Yeah.

He squeezes himself onto the bed, so that his hips are just on the side of the bed. She pulls him in closer, and partly curls what parts of the body she can around him.

Can you, uh –

RACHEL. This is nice.

PETER. Yeah.

RACHEL. I can feel your heartbeat, it's going quick actually…

PETER. Is it?

RACHEL. Yeah. (*Takes his hand and puts it on his heart.*)

PETER. Yeah.

RACHEL. You're nervous, that's all –

> *Beat.*

> (*Soft.*) Do you mind the scar?

PETER. No.

RACHEL. It'll fade. I mean, I'll look the same…

PETER. You're really pretty. You still are.

> *Beat.*

RACHEL. This is nice. I like it like this.

> *She feels her hand around and sort of pats him.*

PETER (*giggle*). Oh. Um. Mr Norris asked if you wanted work set, by the way.

> *She giggles.*

> And Mr Edwards, though he was weird about it, he said I had to talk to him, well, if I wanted to, and that I had to call him Geoff…

RACHEL (*giggle*). Geoff!

PETER (*giggle*). Yeah.

> *Pause. She tries to snuggle up.*

RACHEL. I'm really happy just like this…

PETER. Yeah.

RACHEL. Geoff!

PETER (*giggle*). Yeah.

RACHEL. What did you do?

PETER. I don't know. Ran away.

> *She smiles. Pause, a long luxury pause. They breathe into each other.*

RACHEL. I wish we could just stay like this…

PETER. Yeah.

Pause.

RACHEL (*suddenly whitens*). Peter. Is that… Peter. Have you got an erection?

PETER. No.

He shifts his groin backwards.

RACHEL. Yes. Ow.

PETER. No.

RACHEL. Peter – you can't – ow –

PETER. I can't – I'm sorry –

He moves his arms back, he tries to find space, he can't. She growls like a cat, pure frustration. He's almost in tears.

Sorry – I can't…

RACHEL. I can *feel* it – uh – uh –

He's trying to pull everything away from her.

PETER. Don't, don't, I'm sorry. I'm sorry.

Beat.

I'm sorry.

Beat. He's as far back as he can be, yet he still flurries some more, trying to find more space.

I'm so sorry. Rachel… Rachel…

RACHEL (*half-spoken*). Okay.

Beat. She's struggling to control her tears. He concentrates on holding his stomach in.

PETER. Sorry –

RACHEL. No.

PETER. Sorry, shall I get off –

Beat.

RACHEL. Hold me.

PETER. Sorry. I'm so sorry.

Pause. She moves towards him. He tries to evade as much of her as possible, but she's more aggressive than he is.

Pause.

RACHEL. No. Get off.

PETER. Sorry. I'm really…

He half-falls off the bed in relief.

It's not. It doesn't mean I expect… it's not like a signal or…

Beat. She can't speak. He tries to stand in a way that minimises the erection. He takes another squirt from his inhaler, he's in a panic.

I'm really really sorry, I just don't know what to do… That's all. Sorry.

Beat.

RACHEL (*swallow*). Okay.

PETER. I feel sick. I'm really sorry.

Pause. PETER *can't decide whether to leave or not. He's determined not to look at the door until he does.*

(*Soft, his mouth doesn't work properly.*) I'm not sure what I'm supposed to do…

Pause. He straightens his back, the erection has finally subsided.

Rachel…

Pause.

Rach…

RACHEL (*looks up finally, meets his face*). Yeah?

PETER. Sorry? Sorry.

Blackout.

1.2

21st January.

JAMES and ALICE are beautiful people. RACHEL is enjoying them, despite herself. PETER is a little cluttered. All except RACHEL wear school uniform.

JAMES. … He was having a go and he put his hand down her trousers and he couldn't find what he was looking for so he kept looking and then he put his finger in, but it wasn't the right hole –

RACHEL. What?

JAMES. Went for the pink and potted the brown, Mary Gill, though this isn't from either of them. Anyway, so she slapped him.

ALICE. Did she?

JAMES. Didn't I tell you this? Yeah. Apparently she slapped him.

RACHEL. Mary?

JAMES. Yeah.

ALICE. She's fancied him for ages.

JAMES (*opens his bag and brings out cheap vodka*). Well, he's not going near her now – probably not until he smelt his finger that he realised. (*Takes a swig of the vodka.*) Actually, he smelt his finger and he's either realised, or he thinks she's seriously unwell, can you drink?

RACHEL. Yeah.

PETER. What?

JAMES (*mimicking PETER as he hands her the bottle*). 'What?' Have you got any music?

PETER. James –

RACHEL (*to PETER*). What? (*To JAMES.*) Nothing good.

JAMES (*laughs*). I'll find something.

RACHEL. Okay.

> PETER *sits down on the side of the bed. He turns on the bedside light beside RACHEL, then looks around at the rest of the room and turns the light off again. ALICE smiles at him. RACHEL looks at ALICE. ALICE doesn't know what to say.*

ALICE (*gesturing the vodka bottle*). Can I borrow that?

RACHEL. Yeah.

> ALICE *takes a swig.* PETER *stands up and tucks an errant bit of sheet in, with a complicated smile.*

ALICE. Suzy and Mike have finally got together –

RACHEL. Have they?

ALICE. Yeah.

RACHEL. I don't really know Suzy that well…

ALICE. Oh, she's great, I should introduce you –

RACHEL. Yeah, I've met her.

ALICE. No. I mean, you should, you should definitely come out with us some time –

RACHEL. Okay.

PETER. Girls' night out? You should definitely do that.

ALICE (*swinging a grateful grin in* PETER*'s direction*). So you'll come?

RACHEL. Okay.

ALICE. Brilliant.

JAMES. This is a shit music collection, you know –

PETER. James –

RACHEL. Yeah, I know.

JAMES. Pete, take an interest, mate, sort your girlfriend's music collection out.

RACHEL. Yeah.

JAMES. No, I'm not being serious. Your mum's really lovely, by the way, she tried to invite us to dinner –

RACHEL. Did she?

JAMES. Yeah.

> *Beat.* JAMES *tries to touch* ALICE *surreptitiously.* RACHEL *notices.* ALICE *notices* RACHEL *notice and steps away from her boyfriend's grasp.*
>
> *Pause.* RACHEL *smiles. She looks at* ALICE *directly.* JAMES *notices and takes a step away from* ALICE, *and then, because he doesn't want it to look obvious, he takes another step, and then he walks to the other side of the room.*

This is nice, this room –

ALICE. This is really nice actually –

JAMES (*turning to his girlfriend, all hips*). Which is different from nice how?

ALICE. What?

PETER. By being 'really nice' I think, mate…

JAMES (*small exclusive chuckle*). Okay.

ALICE. We think Mr Taylor might have been sacked.

RACHEL. Yeah?

JAMES. Well. Yeah. Alice thinks he might have touched up Rebecca –

ALICE. She's been telling him about her period.

JAMES. Apparently he's 'really good to talk to'. Which means he's a pervert. I mean, she's got nothing even to talk about neither – though it could be her period, I suppose, if there's some discharge in it – he's a pervert whatever, I think. Anyway, he's off at the moment, someone's taking his lessons –

PETER (*turning to* RACHEL). Are you okay?

RACHEL (*with a funny face*). Yes.

PETER. It's good, isn't it? Having everyone here –

RACHEL. Is it?

JAMES. Leave her alone, mate…

PETER. What?

JAMES (*to* RACHEL). More vodka?

Beat. He takes the vodka from ALICE, *who lets him, and gives it to* RACHEL, *who lets him. She wipes the lid and has a swig.* PETER *then tries to take it from her, and she reluctantly lets him. He puts it on the chest of drawers, away from everyone.*

Oh, and Colin Jackson is coming to school, that's the other thing, to do prize-giving – Nightingale's really excited – it's really funny actually – he's not Colin Jackson, he's 'World-Record-Holder Colin Jackson'. He's given an assembly about you too –

RACHEL. Has he?

JAMES. Yeah.

ALICE. We had a policeman come in and tell us about safety and everything –

RACHEL. Who?

PETER tugs on his asthma inhaler. He looks around to see if anyone's watching him. JAMES moves over towards the vodka.

ALICE. The policeman?

RACHEL. Yeah.

ALICE. I don't know.

RACHEL. Okay.

PETER. I wasn't there, it was just for the girls…

Beat. ALICE walks over to where JAMES is, just because she wants to stand close to him. JAMES picks up a hairclip from the top of RACHEL's chest of drawers, studiously avoiding the vodka. He puts the hairclip down again. He fiddles with one of the drawer knobs, but he doesn't open anything.

JAMES. Everyone's been talking about you…

RACHEL. Saying what?

ALICE. Just loads of nice stuff.

JAMES. Pretending you're their best friend. It was getting boring… I mean, it's stopped now basically…

RACHEL. Yeah?

JAMES. Everyone's been really dumb about it.

RACHEL. Yeah.

Pause. ALICE takes JAMES's hand. PETER moves closer to RACHEL.

JAMES. Has the police said anything?

Beat.

RACHEL. No. Not much. I'm just – we did… a photofit.

JAMES. How come they aren't showing that around the school then?

RACHEL. I don't know.

JAMES. Probably just want to catch him, that's what's wrong with the whole thing actually. They should be showing us and saying, 'Fuck catching him, let's just prevent this happening to more girls.' Shouldn't they?

RACHEL. I don't know.

JAMES. Not my problem, I suppose. How come you don't have a TV up here?

RACHEL. I didn't want one.

JAMES. So what do you do? When Peter's not here –

RACHEL. Oh. I can't remember.

Beat.

ALICE. Okay.

Beat. PETER *wakes up and moves half a step closer to* RACHEL, *both* JAMES *and* ALICE *watch him. Then* RACHEL's *mobile phone goes off. She picks it up and rejects the call.*

PETER. Who was it?

RACHEL. I didn't know the number…

PETER. It could have been the police…

RACHEL. No.

JAMES. Listen to him! All responsible now, are you, Petey? Peter told you about county trials… Baylis thinks he's a shoo-in…

PETER. No. I'm not –

JAMES. He couldn't get picked for the school team before this year. I think he did a soccer-skills thing during the summer and never told anyone –

RACHEL (*to* PETER). You didn't tell me – That's good, isn't it?

JAMES. Yeah. It is.

PETER. It doesn't mean anything.

JAMES. You watch him. He'll get the lead in the musical next –

ALICE (*giggle*). We watched them do the auditions, you could just sit there if you were auditioning too, so we just sat there…

PETER. You auditioned?

JAMES. No, mate, you go for it. It was funny watching though – (*Sings.*) 'Maybe this time…'

ALICE. It was pathetic.

JAMES *checks his watch,* RACHEL *notices him. He notices* RACHEL *noticing him and blushes.*

153

RACHEL. You better go. I'm pretty tired.

PETER. Yeah. She's pretty tired.

> *Beat.* JAMES *shrinks slightly.* ALICE *dwindles too.* RACHEL, *annoyed with* PETER, *tries to help them.*

RACHEL. Going somewhere nice?

ALICE. No. Everyone's just meeting at The Dog and Goat.

RACHEL. Are you going, Peter?

PETER. No.

JAMES. Aren't you? Okay.

> *Pause.*

ALICE. Are you two closer? Would you say? Now this has all happened? I mean, me and Jay got closer just because when he got ill, I went round there a lot. But that wasn't a proper illness…

RACHEL. Yeah?

> *Pause.*

JAMES. We got closer because she let me shag her but she won't say that –

ALICE (*giggles*). Shut up.

> *Pause.* JAMES *moves closer to* ALICE, ALICE *sways towards him.*

JAMES. There's nothing we can do, by the way? Like, you want lifting or anything…

> *Pause.* RACHEL *looks at* PETER *accusingly.*

RACHEL. Where?

JAMES (*looking at* PETER *too. Laughs*). I don't know.

> *Pause.*

PETER. I think everything's fine, isn't it?

RACHEL. Is it?

JAMES (*laying it on thick*). Is it?

PETER. Yeah. I mean, I don't know.

RACHEL. Yeah. It's fine.

PETER. Okay.

> *Blackout.*

1.3

24th January.

PETER *is sitting, watching* RACHEL *sleep. He doesn't move a muscle. He just sits in his seat and watches her. It's dark, we can barely see anything.*

ANGELA *enters ever so quietly.*

ANGELA. She asleep?

PETER. Yeah.

> ANGELA *moves to the bed and sits gently beside her daughter. She traces her daughter's outline with her hand. But she never touches her.* PETER *just watches, unsure what to do.*

ANGELA. How is she?

PETER. Yeah. Okay.

ANGELA. You're speaking quite loudly, Peter –

> *Beat.* PETER *lowers his head slightly.*

> (*Trying to correct herself.*) Arsched says this is all perfectly normal –

PETER. Yeah?

> *Pause. She silently pulls up a chair and sits beside him.*

ANGELA. You know better than any of us really…

PETER. Yeah?

ANGELA. Well, that's a good thing, isn't it? Will you call me Angela, Peter?

PETER. What? Okay.

ANGELA. They all call, and she says she won't have them. All her other friends…

PETER. Yeah?

ANGELA (*gets up from her chair*). Have the police spoken to you?

PETER. No.

ANGELA. I keep phoning them up. I imagine it's really very annoying for them. Rachel doesn't seem that… worried. Still, I suppose that's perfectly natural. She doesn't want me involved. Social services sit with her whenever they come. Arsched says it'll all be okay with that. The police are very kind about it too. I just want him caught, you know.

Pause. ANGELA *circles* RACHEL *slightly, she's now closer to* PETER.

Now. (*Small presumptive sniff.*) Do you... kiss... still?

PETER. What?

ANGELA. I, uh, it's not my business, but I still want her to still be normal... with you... I know she's making you do... you're having to nurse her. You're doing brilliantly.

PETER. Yeah?

ANGELA. Arsched tells me to respect what she wants. But I know I should be up here.

PETER. I'm not, really. I mean, we're pretty normal...

ANGELA (*quiet*). Will you try and get her to talk to me?

PETER. Yeah? I think, I mean, I don't want to upset her...

ANGELA. Okay.

PETER. Sorry. I mean, yeah...

Beat.

ANGELA. It is quite... strange... isn't it – why she wants you here?

PETER. Yeah?

ANGELA. They tell me she can't move her legs because she's afraid of her... vagina. Of the whole... sex, of her sex. And if that's true then why does she want her boyfriend here? I think you're doing brilliantly though... you really are...

ANGELA *gets up and walks to the door.* PETER *takes a tug on his inhaler. The lights start to slowly fade.*

(*Speaks so quietly it's difficult to make out what she says.*) You're right, I don't want her getting upset, if she wakes up... finds me...

PETER. No. I didn't mean that.

ANGELA. No... you're right.

Pause. She's finding it really difficult to leave. PETER *looks round at her.*

I sometimes think we should force her – just tell her they can work – because they can – medically – but then they tell me that this is medical too – her thinking her leg's dead is somehow... medical...

PETER. She's going to get better.

ANGELA. I know...

PETER. No. I mean, you've, uh... I'm going to try really hard...

ANGELA. Okay. Well. Come down when you're ready.

PETER. I'm going to make sure she gets better. I know what I'm doing. Really...

ANGELA. Okay. I'll cook you something if you like.

The lights are in blackout. ANGELA *exits.*

PETER. Okay.

ACT TWO

2.1

30th January.

The lights ping on, full beam. The scene change is instant (there is nothing to change, though perhaps RACHEL*'s duvet has been pulled up over her feet – just slightly).* PETER *is standing where the previous scene left him.*

RACHEL (*soft, she can't get enough liquid in her mouth, every time she opens her mouth we can hear it – a soft shtick on every word*). He had a knife, he said, I didn't see that till – he just told me, I didn't see it till later. And he just stood in the… path, and he said about the knife, and then 'You've got to follow me.' Polite and everything, very… honest. He said I had to follow him. That he wasn't… He wasn't going to be behind me, he was going to be in front of me and that I had to follow him. So I did, he was maybe three or four steps in front and I was just – following – and we came to this small – there was some swings and some – this big – and he took me to basically a shed, I followed him, to, I don't know, a shed, basically, I mean, probably the allotments, but not, definite, and he turned a light on, it was this – bulb – and then, like, undress…

Pause. She paddles backwards with her shoulder, she turns as if to look at him. He turns towards her too. But they don't quite make it. She paddles with her shoulder again.

(*Her voice is full of snot.*) And then he, uh – (*Clears her throat, it doesn't work; clears her throat again.*) I wish I could – I can't even see the inside of… it. I mean, it could be a shed or a… It could have be… They can't even find it.

Pause. Both of them keep very still now, as if being judged.

PETER (*soft, flicking himself out of the softness*). You don't have to – tell me…

RACHEL. I had to stand in there – I had to be slow, taking off the clothes, I can't remember how he said it, but he told me which bits he wanted off first… He spoke really detailed…

Beat.

He said – uh, he wanted my T-shirt off – saying how he wished it was a shirt, he liked buttons... How can I remember this and not the – shed? And then he wouldn't let me take off my underwear for ages because he said he liked that. He kept telling me what he liked. And I threw up sometimes and he made me clean it up with my T-shirt. He tried to do it through my knickers because – and then he asked if it was my first time, saying he was pleased it was him because he could – appreciate it. And he put his fingers all over me, I remember these... They were so scratchy, like, old skin and, he never used his nails.

Pause. She looks up at him, frightened. He takes a tug on his inhaler, she watches him.

Do you want to know the worst bit? Do – you – that sounds such a – but... (*Giggle.*) The worst bit was – was when the doctors examined me afterwards, because then I felt it... all. They put me in this room, they call it a suite but it's a room – the police – and then the doctors come and... They had to – take samples from me – my – me – vagina, my... bum, my mouth, my – they had to take cuttings of my pube... And the doctor had this latex, his breath smelt of latex too – or rubber or whatever it is – like an uncle with his face up close... It felt like the dentist. It was then... after... that I couldn't get off the table, they couldn't get me off. It was then my legs didn't work. And he just smiled and then frowned. And there was this woman, police officer, and she was just sitting there watching it as if he was normal. And that was the... Is that terrible? That that's the... That I think that?

Beat.

Peter?

PETER. I don't... Have you got – is there anything I can ask?

RACHEL. What?

PETER. For – the – is there anything you'd like me to ask? Anything you want me to know but want me to ask the questions for?

RACHEL. What?

PETER. It just feels like you want me to ask something...

RACHEL. No –

PETER. It sounded as if you weren't saying something.

RACHEL. I said everything.

She reaches out a hand to him, but he doesn't meet it. So she turns it into a hand reaching for a cup, she drains it. He walks to the foot of her bed, and pulls the duvet over her toes, before coming back up the bed to stand beside her.

PETER. Shall I get some more water?

Pause. She looks at him carefully.

I'm really pleased you told me. I think it's important. Yeah.

RACHEL. He, uh, he helped me clean up afterwards. He found some – cloth – my T-shirt or… I don't know. I couldn't even feel it but he – I couldn't stop bleeding and he… And then I said that I wouldn't tell anyone, I said I didn't want him to tell anyone, that was so he could believe the lie. Because it was shameful, I said. Because I thought he could kill me otherwise. An' then he took the knife and he said 'Just as a reminder'…

PETER. My / mum…

RACHEL. I told him he had to help me by keeping it a secret, I had blood on my face, and he said he would and he sort of – patted – the side of my – face… and then he started punching where he'd cut, to make sure it scarred, he said… just punching… but the doctors say it'll be okay… and he didn't break anything…

Beat.

PETER. Do you want to… talk… I mean, it must have been pretty bad, so we could – we could talk about this stuff. Just talk it out.

RACHEL. Okay. Aren't we doing that?

PETER. No. Listen, I've been thinking about – I was thinking I should like sit in on your sessions with Arsched – I want to be part of making you better…

RACHEL. Why?

PETER. I just mean, well, I'm here, aren't I?

RACHEL. I know…

PETER. No, I just think I should come along, it's only fair…

RACHEL. Fair?

PETER. No, I mean, really help you. With the police too, I mean, you've told me everything so I could come to that. I know now, I won't judge, I can be a better support than all of them. I mean, it must be hard you saying it all the time and you know that I won't – that I know it now so I could be there – to support you…

RACHEL (*quiet*). But I don't want that.

PETER. It's just that when Mum got sick – I used to go to the therapist's and everything with her all the time. Sometimes they'd talk alone but mostly I'd go in with her – and I was only eight or something then… Just sitting in, you know.

Pause. She picks up a hairbrush from beside her bed and begins to brush her hair. He watches her carefully.

That's why I think I could be helping more… with you…

Pause.

RACHEL. Arsched told me, I'd decided you were safe… I don't know why I did that… sexually, I mean, safe. He reckons I can't move my legs because I said in my head I wanted to be safe from sex. He said I must have decided you were safe too… sexually…

Beat.

PETER. I talked to Alice actually, and she – before, I haven't told her the stuff that – I mean, she's great to talk to – I mean, I just think talking it out helps, I think I could really help…

RACHEL. What did you say to her?

PETER. I don't know. I didn't know most of the stuff, did I? Just, I don't know, how I was feeling… I don't know. I mean –

RACHEL. I'm not jealous, Peter. I don't think you're her type –

PETER. No… Look, she really likes you – she said how much she liked you, when she, uh –

RACHEL. Peter, that's just something someone like her would say –

Pause. PETER *shifts his chair forward, it makes a funny noise, he looks down to where the noise is coming from, he can't work it out.*

PETER. Well, that's not important – I want to be involved, that's all I'm saying, I'd be really good at helping you, I could really support you. (*Spilling.*) Rachel, what happened – with the – I know we didn't talk about it – but I don't want you to worry about that. I can control that.

RACHEL. What?

PETER. I just was lying really close to you – and you're really pretty – it won't happen again.

RACHEL. It doesn't matter.

PETER. It won't happen again, I know what I'm doing, just – let me be part of it…

Knock on the door.

ANGELA. Kids?

RACHEL. Mum…

ANGELA (*opening the door*). Hi. Is this okay?

RACHEL. No.

ANGELA. I've got your washing –

RACHEL says nothing. ANGELA carries the basket of washing over to RACHEL's chest of drawers.

So what have you two been up to –

RACHEL. Peter can put that away…

ANGELA. I'm sure Peter doesn't want to put your underwear away for you…

PETER. I don't mind.

Beat.

ANGELA. Hello, Peter.

PETER. Hi. Do you want me to –

RACHEL. See? He can do it.

Pause. ANGELA puts the basket down on top of the chest of drawers.

ANGELA. I can't just sit downstairs –

RACHEL (*exploding*). SO GET YOUR OWN LIFE!

ANGELA. Rachel –

RACHEL. WHAT?

Pause. ANGELA thinks a moment, and then leaves.

ANGELA. I'll see you downstairs, Peter…

RACHEL. Will you?

Pause. RACHEL listens for the footsteps going down the stairs.

She's so… big, all the time… and then being so 'I'll see you downstairs, Peter' making herself sound big… You better go.

PETER. What?

RACHEL. I want to be on my own for a little bit.

PETER. Why?

Pause. He walks over to her chest of drawers and starts looking at unpacking the laundry. He picks up a pair of knickers.

RACHEL. I mean it, Peter…

He puts down the pair of knickers.

PETER. But I want to stay up here…

RACHEL. Well, I can't leave, can I?

PETER. What?

RACHEL (*mimicking*). 'What?'

Pause.

PETER. I just think you're being unfair, to me, to Angela…

RACHEL. 'Angela'?

PETER. What? Listen. As long as I haven't done anything wrong…

RACHEL. 'Angela'?

Pause. She touches her scar.

PETER. Look, today was a good day, okay? Let's not ruin things by fighting about things that aren't really important – I think – I'm going to stay for a bit…

Pause. She pushes her arm under her pillow.

Are you okay then?

Blackout.

2.2

2nd February.

ALICE *is sitting in the room. She's a bit fidgety and entirely different without* JAMES *to chaperone her speaking.*

ALICE. But then we talked all about that, and he didn't even like that, he thought I liked it, which is why he invited me. Or he said that, I'm not sure if I believe him really –

RACHEL. Okay.

ALICE. He could be lying because he doesn't want us to split up, so he wants to pretend there isn't a problem. Anyway, we're going to try spending more time together –

Pause.

Your face is healing well, isn't it?

RACHEL (*wants to touch her scar, but doesn't*). Yeah.

ALICE. Do you want me to bring some make-up? Cover-stick, that sort of thing…

RACHEL. No.

ALICE. My mum said she wanted to buy a present for you, when she heard about it, so I could get her to pay.

RACHEL. No. Is Peter okay? At school?

ALICE. Yeah, he's great. Everyone's treating him a bit like – like he's special, because of what happened and because he's being, you know, so supportive for you. I mean, he is special, isn't he? He was brilliant to talk to about the whole James thing – I mean, because he understands what James is really like, you know –

RACHEL. Yeah.

ALICE. I mean, they're not getting on great at the moment, but they've been friends for so long, I mean, far longer than either of us have been around – with them –

RACHEL. Yeah.

ALICE. So they'll be friends again, though my mum said, when I talked to her about it, that she doesn't really know that many friends from school, which I found really weird. It'll be quite funny really if we stop being friends and then we meet up again later, at a reunion or whatever. Though she said she hadn't had any school reunions either. We've got to have a school reunion, I think. In ten years or whatever, I mean… I mean, my mum isn't even bothering with the website thing or anything like that, but I'd *love* to know what everyone's doing in ten years, it'd be so interesting…

RACHEL. Yeah.

ALICE. You think so?

RACHEL. Is Peter the same though – as he was?

ALICE. Yeah, I mean, everyone's really giving him respect. I mean, I'm sure he'd like it better if you were around, but you still get to see each other loads, don't you?

RACHEL. Not the way we were… no.

ALICE. Does it seem really long ago now?

RACHEL. What?

ALICE. Well, when it all started –

RACHEL. When I was… attacked?

ALICE. Yeah.

RACHEL. No.

ALICE. It seems really long ago to me –

RACHEL. Does it?

ALICE. I suppose you've been here mostly. But Peter said you might come down for the trials –

RACHEL. Did he?

ALICE. Yeah. James is going now, having a go now, so I'm going to go too. Did you hear about all that?

RACHEL. What?

ALICE. Mr Baylis was a wanker and said that he shouldn't do the trials, but James thought about it and said he was at least as good as the other players going, and it's open trials anyway, it's not even proper. Did Peter tell you about that?

RACHEL. No.

ALICE. I think he's pleased, that James is going –

RACHEL. Probably.

ALICE. I thought about not going – because of what we decided – about me not having to be with him all the time – doing girls' nights and stuff like that – which you have to come to, by the way – and then I thought that I'd actually quite like to see the trials – because when stuff like that's important, you know – I mean, you're going even and you're basically here most of the time –

RACHEL. If I'm better –

ALICE. Really? Oh, Peter said it like it was definite. He said you were getting so much better so quickly. He said he could almost see it – how much better you were getting. Or that may be me thinking that, and he didn't say that at all. I don't think Peter says things like that – but he definitely said you were getting tonnes better. Well. It doesn't matter. It's funny, isn't it? How we never used to be friends – I mean, even with James and Peter being –

RACHEL. We don't need to be friends.

Pause.

ALICE. Are you seeing a psychiatrist?

RACHEL. Psychologist.

ALICE. I had a feeling about that. What's that like? That's not rude, is it – it's just I knew a girl – who had to use one. A cousin of my mum's. She fell in love with hers.

RACHEL. Arsched's fifty.

ALICE (*laugh*). Oh. Okay. Oh, I'm doing the musical *Cabaret*. I got a part.

RACHEL. Did you?

ALICE. Yeah, weird, isn't it?

RACHEL. No.

ALICE. I just went afterwards… don't tell James… It's not a big part… well, it's quite big.

RACHEL. Okay.

ALICE. He's waiting downstairs, by the way. Do you want him to come up?

RACHEL. Who?

ALICE. James. Just don't tell him about the musical.

RACHEL. He's downstairs…

ALICE. Don't worry, he won't come up…

RACHEL. What?

ALICE. Or I could go? You know, if you're bored or anything, I don't mind – It's weird, isn't it? Because basically I only normally see you with James and Peter – He's really sweet, you know, James –

RACHEL. Yeah.

ALICE. I know you don't like him but I think the four of us could be really good friends, it's just you've got to catch him when he's being funny. I mean, he likes you, he thinks you're really nice –

RACHEL. When did you lose... your virginity?

ALICE. Oh.

RACHEL. It's just – I know I was later than everyone else...

ALICE. Not that later – I mean... Everyone lies about that stuff, don't they? I know Michelle Milsom didn't lose hers at fourteen and she says she did.

RACHEL. I hadn't – before the...

ALICE. Oh.

RACHEL. Yeah. I suppose, at least it's over with...

ALICE. It feels odd, doesn't it? I mean, obviously it was different and everything...

RACHEL. Yeah, it is.

Beat.

ALICE. Can I do anything?

RACHEL. What?

ALICE. No. It doesn't matter.

Pause. JAMES appears in the doorway, neither of them notice him.

JAMES. Your mum wanted to ask if we wanted dinner, she's going to cook... But I said we probably should go... Hi. Rachel. I mean – do you want to go straight away or, you know, I could chat a bit...

RACHEL. Hi.

JAMES. Yeah. Peter said you just wanted to chat to Alice really...

ALICE. No. He just said you wanted to talk to a girl...

RACHEL. Did he?

JAMES. Yeah. I got that actually – I mean, Peter probably talks about the same stuff I do. I mean, you and Alice have probably got more in common.

ALICE. Yeah.

Pause. RACHEL *squeezes her head around to look at* ALICE.

RACHEL. He asked you to come?

ALICE. I wanted to – and then he said you could do with talking to a girl, and I thought that was – brilliant. Though James wasn't supposed to come up...

JAMES. I'm allowed to come up!

RACHEL. He shouldn't have asked you.

ALICE. I was really pleased though.

Pause.

JAMES. He's not about then?

RACHEL. No. He's doing some football thing...

JAMES. Is he?

RACHEL. Yeah. I mean... That's what he said...

JAMES (*laugh*). Well, it's not another girl...

RACHEL. Yeah, I know...

JAMES. He's probably getting you a present or something. (*Laugh.*) Or doing the football thing, of course...

RACHEL. Yeah.

JAMES. It's probably a football thing. I just hadn't heard about it.

RACHEL. Yeah.

JAMES. Did he... get picked?

RACHEL. For what?

JAMES. Okay. Doesn't matter...

RACHEL. Okay.

Pause.

JAMES. He's doing alright, though, with you? Being supportive and everything?

RACHEL. Yeah.

JAMES. Good. I was a bit worried he was going to be a wanker.

Blackout.

168

2.3

7th February.

RACHEL is asleep. ANGELA is sitting beside her. PETER enters with two cups of tea, one of which he puts beside ANGELA's chair, on the floor. He has to bend down far too far to get it there, making a hugely concerted effort not to spill anything, whilst still holding the other cup, it looks quite comical.

ANGELA. Thanks, love.

Pause. PETER sits down.

PETER. Is she… uh?

ANGELA (*can't take her eyes off her daughter*). Her dad always used to let her fall asleep on the sofa. Watching the TV, sometimes, not all the time. He only did it because he liked carrying her upstairs to bed.

PETER. Yeah?

ANGELA. They looked very… gentle together…

PETER. I wish I'd met him…

ANGELA. Don't – there's something about remembering that always makes you remember it better. I remember – after Ian… died – I wrote a note to myself saying don't think he was brilliant –

PETER. Yeah?

ANGELA. You've got to remember that, otherwise you didn't love them. It must be the same with you and Rachel, you might only remember how great it was before… well. Whatever it was before… But you certainly seemed – I thought you were a good boyfriend.

PETER. Okay.

ANGELA. I phoned your mum, to say how great you're being, to check you're okay at home, because this must be difficult for you. Well, just so she knows…

PETER. Yeah, she said. You didn't need to do that…

ANGELA. She seemed pleased.

PETER. She was okay?

ANGELA. Yeah.

PETER. Okay, I thought she'd been rude.

ANGELA. No, very pleasant.

PETER. She sounded like she'd been rude, when she told me about it.

ANGELA. No. She's had some difficult times... from what Rachel told me. Not much, obviously.

PETER. Not that difficult.

Pause.

I phoned the police...

ANGELA. Did you?

PETER. To ask if I could help. They said no.

ANGELA. Okay.

PETER. Yeah, I mean, they said it was going fine.

ANGELA. It's not.

PETER. Well, I'm not sure you know that...

ANGELA. Sorry?

PETER. I think we're – me and Rachel are doing well – I mean, making progress –

ANGELA. Good, I hope I'm part of it too –

PETER. Yeah, but I'm pretty sure we're on the right track – I mean, me and Rachel have been talking quite seriously – I really feel we're getting somewhere – I mean, don't get any hopes up – but, you know, it's a start.

ANGELA. Good. That's – What have you been talking about?

PETER. There is something – I mean, you do come up quite a lot, and I think that's part of the problem you two are having –

ANGELA. You think I'm seeing too much of my daughter?

PETER. No. That doesn't matter that much. I suppose I'm just feeling very confident about it really – you know, I feel great about it really... I think I'm really helping – I'm, um, yeah.

ANGELA. Well. That's great.

RACHEL. I'm not asleep.

Beat.

ANGELA. Did we wake you, love?

RACHEL. No.

Pause.

ANGELA. Do you want me to go?

RACHEL. Put on the light.

PETER puts the bedside lamp on.

PETER. Hi.

Pause. RACHEL's face adjusts to the light.

RACHEL. Do you do this every night?

ANGELA. No.

RACHEL. This isn't a hospital. You shouldn't do that.

ANGELA. Okay.

RACHEL. I mean it…

ANGELA. Okay.

Pause. RACHEL touches her scar, as if to reaffirm it's still there.

RACHEL (*soft*). What were you saying… about Dad?

ANGELA. Oh. That. Well, I don't know if you remember him, carrying you up to bed.

RACHEL. I remember the game we used to do – 'Sack of Potatoes'.

ANGELA. Yes. That's right. He would get you in your sleeping bag –

RACHEL. No, he'd put me in there and then he'd put me on his back, in the bag, and go running around the room, bouncing me off anything and then he'd put real salt in the bag and shake it, and then he'd do this thing where he'd pretend he didn't even like potatoes, so he'd tickle me.

PETER. Yeah?

RACHEL. He used to do an accent…

ANGELA. I did it too…

RACHEL. Okay. Do it now.

ANGELA. I can't remember how it goes.

RACHEL. I think Peter thinks it was better that Dad died. Because his didn't, his just fucked off.

171

PETER. No.

Pause.

ANGELA. Are you okay?

RACHEL. I don't even like *him* when you're here... I remember you, before, and you were so not like any of this... You were just much better before you became such a wanker.

ANGELA. Rachel...

RACHEL. Don't pretend you're not pleased, Mum, you've got no reason to be jealous now. He's just as crap as you are.

ANGELA. Rachel, don't be silly. I don't understand what you're saying.

RACHEL. I knew you were the worst one before, Mum, and now I'm not so sure. Listen to him.

PETER. I wasn't saying anything...

RACHEL. I'VE BEEN LISTENING TO YOU! I listened to you. You were telling her all you'd done for me, like it was some kind of an achievement.

ANGELA. It is, if you're getting better –

RACHEL. BUT I'M NOT! Am I? Where are my fucking legs if I am getting better?

ANGELA. Rachel, it'll take time. Be fair.

RACHEL. NEITHER OF YOU ARE DOING ANYTHING!

ANGELA. I'd like to –

RACHEL. BUT YOU'RE FUCKING TALKING! I should go to sleep now...

Pause.

ANGELA. Perhaps that is for the best.

PETER. Yeah.

RACHEL (*dangerous*). What?

Pause.

ANGELA. Do you want that light still on?

RACHEL. I can turn it off...

ANGELA. Sure?

RACHEL (*demonstrates*). My hand can reach, thanks...

172

ANGELA. I don't even know what we've done…

Pause. ANGELA exits, PETER follows her.

PETER (*to* RACHEL). Bye.

ANGELA (*to* RACHEL). I love you.

RACHEL looks to where her mum just left, and then turns off the light.

Pause. She shifts and looks in the opposite direction.

She reaches a hand back and turns the light on again. She keeps staring away from the door.

Blackout.

ACT THREE

3.1

11th February.

PETER *puts his arms around* RACHEL *and pulls her up the bed. This is something they've done thousands of times now. She gets there and takes a breath and so does he.*

RACHEL. I wanted to be a nurse once.

PETER. Did you?

RACHEL. It was when I decided all jobs were selfish, because my mum was switching. I wanted to be a nurse or a police officer because they'd be the jobs I didn't want to do ever.

PETER. Really?

> *Pause.*

> (*Appraises what he is going to do.*) If we, um, twist you round, so that you'll be leaning against the – bedhead and then we put your feet on the ground. It's okay…

RACHEL. If it hurts, I want you to keep going anyway.

PETER. Okay.

> *Pause. A moment's indecision, and then he gets to work. He twists her around, he puts her feet so they can touch the ground. This leaves her with her body cuddling up against the headboard of the bed. Her feet are floppy and useless, her back is twisted.*

> I wanted to be a politician.

RACHEL. What?

PETER. Yeah, I know. But my mum kept this badge I had made. I found it, recently, I mean, really recently – I was going to bring it in for you to look at.

RACHEL. But you changed your mind –

PETER. Yeah, I decided against it, I don't know why – I don't know, it's just a badge –

RACHEL. Who were you standing for? On the badge?

PETER (*throat laugh*). The Peter Party.

RACHEL. Really?

PETER. That's what the badge said –

RACHEL (*giggle*). What were your policies?

PETER. I don't think I had those. I think it was just 'vote for me, I'll make all the decisions when I have to', I think I mainly liked how the politicians dressed… The suits, you know…

RACHEL (*giggle*). Brilliant.

Pause. He sizes her up.

(*Looking at his anxiety.*) I think you should just keep going.

PETER. Okay.

PETER *faces her like a weightlifter, full-on and strong, he pulls her hard up by her armpits, her feet are like puppets' feet, they don't find ground.*

(*Full of strain.*) Uh –

He lets her back down again, he has to try hard to not let his momentum cause him to fall into her. She tries to remain sitting, she doesn't want to go back to lying down. But this means as soon as he gets her down, she starts slipping off the bed, she can't get hold of enough of her headboard. She can't use her feet to arrest her ascent, and her back is exhausted, she makes a small squeak from her mouth as she slips.

PETER *catches her, or half-catches her, and part of her stays on the bed, and slowly, inch by inch, she regains balance and she's sitting again. Or grasping onto the headboard anyway.*

Pause. They both try and regain sense.

Pause. PETER takes a tug on his inhaler.

RACHEL. Okay. Again?

PETER. Um –

RACHEL. If you're – we should –

PETER. Really?

RACHEL. Yeah.

PETER. Okay.

He heaves her up by her armpits and takes the full weight of her on his body. His body isn't vertical, it's half-vertical, with his arse sticking out almost as a ballast. He grabs her around

175

the waist, they're stuck in a horrible position. She is standing against him, she is totally leaning on him, but she's upright. This is an enormous strain for both of them. Her legs don't work to any degree.

(*Everything about him is strained.*) Okay?

RACHEL. Yeah.

PETER. Sure?

RACHEL (*trying not to cry*). Yeah.

PETER. You think… can you try… standing…

RACHEL. No.

PETER. Okay, time to get down…

He starts to waddle her back to the bed. He's using all his strength to lift her. But he can't move her far enough or fast enough. In a series of disjointed manoeuvres he puts her down on the floor. She makes another squeaking noise as he does. They haven't made it back to the bed. She lies on the floor, he hovers somewhere close.

(*Desperately out of breath.*) Sorry.

RACHEL (*exhausted too*). Okay.

He takes a squirt on his inhaler.

No rush, we can stay like this, I like it here…

PETER *coughs, he's exhausted. Pause.*

Can I lie in your lap? To get my head up…

PETER. Yeah?

RACHEL. Okay?

He changes to a sitting position, and helps her put her head on his lap, he leans against the wall. Finally, they've found a comfortable pose, and they both relax as they realise that fact. They look nice together. PETER *coughs again and touches his chest where it hurts, but then he smiles.*

Can you reach my knee?

PETER. Yeah.

RACHEL. Will you pinch it? Don't say when?

She covers her face with her hands. PETER *is slightly surprised. He thinks and then he moves to tweak her knee cautiously.*

(As he hovers his hand above, he doesn't make it.) Then?

PETER. No.

RACHEL. Try again…

> PETER *moves quickly and tweaks her knee.*

I could feel your arm move…

PETER. Okay.

> *Pause. She slumps into his lap.*

RACHEL. I think we should go on a date.

PETER. What?

RACHEL. Just to the cinema, or ice-skating, or dinner. Or a boat trip, just a canoe or… Somewhere nice, I think you should start saving up for it now. Sell all the boxes of chocolates people have sent me.

PETER. Okay.

RACHEL. Yeah? Just somewhere nice, it doesn't have to be expensive, and I mean that – about the chocolates –

PETER. I think your mum will pay actually, she keeps trying to thrust money down my throat –

RACHEL *(keeping positive)*. Okay.

PETER. Yeah.

RACHEL. When we got together – did you think we'd last?

PETER. Yeah.

RACHEL. Good.

PETER. Yeah, I mean, how long?

RACHEL. How long did you think?

PETER. I was really chuffed when it happened though – I mean, you're really pretty. You still are.

> *She reaches her hand up past her scar, towards his throat.*

RACHEL. Bring your – I want to touch your face…

> *He bullet-laughs.*

I do. Can I?

PETER. Yeah.

> *He moves his face down, she gently manipulates her hands over it.*

RACHEL (*moves her hands down over his shoulders, rubbing them*). Do you like this?

PETER. Yeah.

> *Pause. She smiles at him strangely.*
>
> (*Hmmph-laugh.*) What?

RACHEL. Bring your head down. Please. Peter.

PETER. I'm really sweaty...

> *He does, she holds onto his head with the back of her hand, again he's stuck in an odd position, their faces close together.*
>
> *Pause. She takes his hand.*

RACHEL. Smile.

> PETER *does.*
>
> Bring your face in, I wanted to see your smile really closer. Over my eyes. I want to smell your breath –

PETER (*trying to withdraw*). No.

RACHEL (*keeping him held in*). Come on...

PETER. No.

RACHEL (*trying to pull his head down even closer*). Come on...

PETER (*really struggling quite hard*). Please. Ow!

RACHEL (*trying to pull her face up to meet his*). Come on...

PETER (*forcibly dislocates her*). What's the *matter* with you...

> *Pause.*

RACHEL. I want you to give me a bed bath –

PETER. What?

RACHEL. I'll tell you what to do.

> *Pause.*

PETER. I think I should get you back on the bed.

RACHEL. Not yet.

> *Pause. A hoover starts on the stairs. As they talk, it slowly approaches the door, doing a stair at a time. RACHEL acts like she doesn't notice, but the hoover makes PETER even more nervous.*
>
> Will you give me a bed bath?

PETER. No. Of course not. Who normally does it? I'll get her.

RACHEL. Why?

Beat. The hoover is fast approaching.

PETER. The nurse or your mum should do it. Bath you.

RACHEL. I don't want them to.

PETER. When's the nurse next coming?

RACHEL. I don't want her to.

PETER. Then why do you want me to?

RACHEL. Because you're my boyfriend.

Pause. PETER half-stutters out a laugh.

You don't apologise much any more.

PETER. What?

RACHEL. You don't say sorry much any more.

PETER. Yeah?

RACHEL. Why does no one behave like I want them to…

PETER. I think I do, actually…

RACHEL. You're starting to smell like her too.

PETER. It smells in here actually…

RACHEL. Then give me my bed bath! Do you not want to see me?

Beat. The hoover is getting closer and closer.

You don't want to touch me… see my… see me.

PETER. No, I just think your mum would really like that.

RACHEL. I don't want my mum to perve on me.

Pause. The hoover switches off. RACHEL smiles at that, and then frowns back at PETER. They don't say anything for a bit, and when they do, they speak quietly, as if someone's listening.

PETER. I should get you back on the bed.

RACHEL. I like it here.

PETER starts to manipulate her up. RACHEL resists as much as she can.

No, Peter.

PETER (looking towards the door). SH!

RACHEL (*pushing his body hard away*). NO!

> *He gives up. He looks carefully at the door. Footsteps are heard going down the stairs.*

PETER (*quiet and vicious*). You just want to stay on the floor?

RACHEL. Yes!

> *Pause.*

It's normal to want to touch me…

PETER (*boiling hot*). I'm just like your mum / anyway…

RACHEL. That's what the problem is?

PETER. You said I was fucking useless…

RACHEL. So give me a bath!

PETER. Why did you say that to her like that?

RACHEL. You care what she thinks?

PETER. WE WERE GETTING BETTER!

RACHEL. WE FUCKING WEREN'T!

PETER. I WAS HELPING YOU!

RACHEL. FUCK OFF!

PETER. Look. *Look*, let's get you *back* on the *bed*…

RACHEL. I don't want that.

> *He starts to lift her.*

I DON'T WANT THAT!

> *She pushes her hand up into his face. He keeps on trying to drag her up. She forces a hand into his eye, all the time wriggling her shoulders away from him.*

PETER. Ow!

> *They size each other up, and then PETER tries to lift her again, less apologetically this time, by her shoulders and elbows and whatever else he can manage. She grabs a handful of his hair, pulls herself up to his level and she half-headbutts him. They grapple.*

RACHEL (*quiet, concentrated on the effort*). Fucking…

> *She manages to hit his head against the side of the bed. Then she does it again, and it's harder this time. He pushes her down onto the floor, hard, with the flat of his hand. She bites his hand, and then tears at his hair and sticks her*

elbow in his eye. He hits her down (he doesn't punch, it's with the flat of his hand – he is determined to use the flat of his hand wherever possible). She tries to tear at him again, she scratches his eye.

PETER. OW!

She tries to pull at him again. He pushes hard, crack, against the floor – and holds her there. Pinning her with his weight.

STOP IT!

She stops, like a toddler might stop. She doesn't seem to understand what's going on, she just knows she's been hurt. He dislocates himself away from her, pulls himself up to sitting position. She's still lying on the floor. He fiddles in his pocket and takes another tug on his inhaler. He coughs repeatedly, and phlegm comes into his mouth, which he then swallows. She doesn't say anything. It's ages before he speaks.

I… just… think it's not good… on the floor.

Pause.

RACHEL. I've worked out – I'd cover everything he could breathe with – his mouth and – you can do ears too, breathe through ears too. So I'd – just leave his nose. And then I'd stand there and I'd just watch him, tied up with tape over his mouth and his ears and anything he can breathe by. I don't know whether you can breathe through the eyes – I was quite surprised about the ear thing. And I'd have a hammer with me, I'd just sit there mostly, but I'd have a hammer. And every now and again I'd just tap him, his nose, with the hammer, not to break it, just to remind him that I had it, and he'd know that he could only breathe out of his nose, because his mouth and ears are covered, so I'd just keep reminding him of it. And I'd tap it harder and harder but still tapping. Then I'd hit it harder, just so it'd sting or something, just so he really knew. It'd probably be really difficult for him to breathe then, but it'd come back to normal and we'd both wait for that, him and me. Just until it's completely right again. Then I'd break it. He'd probably still be able to breathe then but it'd hurt all the time. Then I'd hit it again until it was flat, his nose, and maybe that'd make him unconscious, the pain, or maybe he'd suffocate. But sometimes I think he's not too bad. I mean, just mixed up a bit, like you. Will you – bring your head down?

Pause.

I think I smell. I can smell myself, Peter. I can smell me, okay? My... I want you to wash me, I want you to see me.

PETER. Anyone can get you clean, if you smell... you don't smell...

Pause. PETER *scratches his hand and touches his eye gingerly. He starts to cry.*

(*Sniff.*) Why... Why did you follow him?

Beat.

No... I'm not accusing, I know there's a reason. If we're being honest.

Pause. PETER *stops crying.*

RACHEL. Will you touch my scar?

PETER (*the phlegm's back in his throat*). What?

RACHEL. To see if it hurts, it doesn't if I touch it, but I can never tell if that means anything...

PETER *bravely reaches out and touches it. She closes her eyes while he does.*

I was raped.

PETER. I know that. Look, I, uh, I think we share this... don't we?

RACHEL. Share what?

PETER. I just think if I don't understand something, I should ask.

RACHEL. Will you go away, Peter?

Beat.

I want you to go.

PETER. Fuck it. Sure.

RACHEL. Yeah?

PETER. You want me to go?

RACHEL. I don't want you to be so fucking gay about it as well.

Pause.

He quivers a moment, and then he leaves.

She listens to him go down the stairs. She tries to count his descent, under her breath.

She finishes counting, she reaches twenty-one, she scratches the top of her arm.

She does nothing.

She hardly moves a muscle, she does nothing, she just lies there.

She counts to twenty-one again.

She gently fiddles with her eye, before reassuming neutral.

She smoothes down her arm.

She thinks. She looks at the side of the bed, and thinks about crawling up it.

She changes her mind, and puts her hand numbly inside her knickers.

She brings it out, checking to see if there's blood on it. There doesn't seem to be.

She smells her hand. She crumples her face as if ready to cry, but she doesn't.

She lies back, she tries to lie back as far as she can. But there isn't far to go.

She smells her hand again. This time there's more efficiency to how she does it.

She looks at her hand and traces the lines on her palm.

She scratches her hair.

She lies and waits.

She just lies there. Perfectly neutral.

An unmoving heavy mass. On the floor. Blackout.

3.2

14th February.

RACHEL is back in bed and is being helped onto the bedpan by ANGELA. RACHEL pushes her knickers down to her mid-thighs, she's getting quite accomplished at this. Again it takes ages for RACHEL to start. There is a wheelchair leaning against the wall of the room.

RACHEL. Ow –

> *ANGELA lifts RACHEL up some more, to make sure she's firmly over the bedpan.*

ANGELA. When we get the wheelchair working, we'll be able to get you into the toilet.

> *RACHEL says nothing.*

> I'm your mother. It affects me too... I'm going to keep coming back until you're used to me...

RACHEL. Do you want me to kill myself?

ANGELA (*wiping something away with her shoulder, as she tightens her grip on RACHEL's bum*). I keep thinking I've let you down...

RACHEL. I just don't like you here.

ANGELA. Why? Why can't we talk about this? I want to...

RACHEL. Because I DON'T WANT TO.

ANGELA. Okay.

> *Pause.*

> They keep telling me – I phone Arsched – and he says, ask yourself the question 'What can I give this person?' And, uh... that I have to tell you that whatever response you have as a – survivor – is normal and I have to respect that... So I have to just have to be your – I just have to obey you until you change...

RACHEL. Okay.

ANGELA. Rachel, when your dad died...

RACHEL. I don't want to talk about that.

ANGELA. Okay.

> *Pause.*

Okay.

Pause. ANGELA *scratches her ear. Pause.*

Did I do something wrong?

RACHEL. Yes.

ANGELA. When?

RACHEL. The whole thing, okay?

ANGELA. They told me on the phone – they asked me 'Have you ever talked about sex with her?'

RACHEL. No –

ANGELA. It felt like they were accusing – but they said they weren't and I thought all that was done at school now – well, I know we needed to talk about it, but you were never an easy person to talk to – I mean – but if we had talked about it then it might have meant we could talk about this –

RACHEL. Wait –

Pause.

RACHEL *starts to pee. This time the dribble is not so painful. It sounds almost normal.*

She farts accidentally. They both keep very still.

They wait for more.

It doesn't come.

ANGELA. I want to talk to you about it, Rachel.

RACHEL (*muffled*). No.

ANGELA. Just tell me what happened.

RACHEL. NO!

ANGELA. Who would do that to a little girl?

RACHEL. I'm not a little girl.

ANGELA. I think –

RACHEL (*turning as far as she can towards her mum*). I DON'T CARE.

Pause. A final dribble, RACHEL *makes a slight growling noise, this takes some effort.*

ANGELA *waits for more,* RACHEL *concentrates on her bladder.*

There's nothing left.

You can go, Mum…

ANGELA. Have you finished?

RACHEL. Yes.

ANGELA. You just wanted a wee, did you…

Beat. RACHEL says nothing.

ANGELA checks she's steady and then hands her the toilet paper. She attempts to break the paper off for her daughter, but is stopped from doing so.

RACHEL uses it aggressively. She dumps the paper in the pan, this causes an involuntary spasm in her back.

ANGELA doesn't notice RACHEL's pain.

RACHEL refocuses on her mother. She pulls up her own knickers.

RACHEL. I hate you doing this… At least Peter didn't like doing it…

ANGELA. Let's just make this easy…

RACHEL is helped off the bedpan. ANGELA carries it out of the room. Having a quick glance at it as she does.

RACHEL waits in silence, she keeps entirely still. She tries not to blink.

ANGELA re-enters, she's now washed the bedpan. She puts it back under the bed and picks up RACHEL's used dinner tray and carries it out.

It was nice, that, wasn't it?

RACHEL. If Peter comes back, you're not to say anything, yeah? If he is –

ANGELA. About what?

RACHEL. About anything, Mum. I don't want you to speak to him at all. He's my friend.

ANGELA (*slumping slightly*). Okay.

RACHEL doesn't say anything, despite ANGELA's pathetic eyes. So ANGELA exits.

Nothing. A big crowd of it.

Nothing.

More nothing. RACHEL *tries not to move. She has a system worked out for her first few moments of peace. It's a tried-and-tested system and generally involves anaesthetising herself with great big silences. Blackout.*

3.3

20th February.

ALICE *is sitting there diligently.* RACHEL *has her back turned to her.*

ALICE. Have you been reading anything?

RACHEL. No.

ALICE. We've got this crap book we've got to read for English. What do you do then? Most of your time? Without a TV. I mean, when you're here.

RACHEL. You think I leave at night?

ALICE. What?

RACHEL. What?

    Pause.

    You think I leave at night?

ALICE. Are your feet getting better then?

RACHEL. What?

ALICE. I don't understand.

RACHEL. You said 'when I'm here'.

ALICE. What?

RACHEL. When am I not?

ALICE. No. I just… Have I said something wrong?

    RACHEL *turns over, this takes some effort, to face* ALICE.

    Um. The musical is going well. I've got promoted.

RACHEL. Okay.

ALICE. I still haven't told James though, isn't that pathetic? Still, I've been thinking a lot about that, since we spoke, and we just aren't that kind of couple, you know. I mean, he's amazing in bed. I mean, actually, isn't it funny that that's embarrassing? I mean, it wasn't great to start with but now it's nice – loving, you know. It's funny. I don't know. Have you seen Peter?

RACHEL (*laugh, funny voice*). I thought I left him with you.

ALICE. No. He's not in school. James went to see him, but he wasn't in. His mum was a bitch to James actually. Told him off for leaving his bike on the lawn.

Pause.

Is that a wheelchair?

RACHEL. Yes.

ALICE. Oh. Suzy's split up with –

RACHEL. – I don't know them.

ALICE. Um. I wasn't sure how long to leave it before coming back. I wasn't…

RACHEL. Yeah. What do you want to talk about?

ALICE. There's nothing… I can do or anything…

RACHEL. Do you know why my real friends aren't here? Because they asked, and I said no. They asked me whether I wanted them here, and I didn't…

ALICE. Do you want me to tell them to come over?

RACHEL. Did you not hear what I said?

ALICE. You sounded like you'd changed your mind.

RACHEL. You want to make an announcement in assembly, don't you? 'Rachel's ready to receive visitors she was nasty to before. She's okay now.'

ALICE. No. I just thought you might want someone round here…

RACHEL. Why? To entertain me…

ALICE. Well, it's not exactly entertaining you, is it? It's just chatting really…

RACHEL. Depends how clever you are…

ALICE (*completely crushed – with a big smile*). Have I done something wrong? I mean, I liked it… here…

RACHEL. We don't have anything to talk about…

ALICE. Yeah, but we can talk about loads of stuff, music, things like that…

RACHEL. I don't *like* that stuff…

ALICE. James isn't going to come barging in again. I had such a go at him about that.

Beat.

When you said – about the virginity thing – I wasn't really – when I, it wasn't like he asked or anything. I mean, it wasn't bad or anything like that, but he just didn't really ask. And it is entirely different, I mean, James, I'm in love with him, so when he did it, it was fine. And I didn't say no or anything like that, because it was really surprising, and I had to go and get the twenty-four-hour thing. But it was so weird, you know? I wanted to say, that I wasn't sure when I was going to – I wanted to save it a little bit too. I don't think it's that odd really, wanting to stay a virgin, I mean, I'd have quite liked that. He said afterwards it was an accident, well, he said it like I made a mistake but then we kept doing it after that. Like that had been the first for real rather than an accident.

Pause.

RACHEL. Do you want me to say something?

ALICE. No.

RACHEL. Good.

Pause.

ALICE (*with honour*). You still want me to go?

RACHEL. Yes.

ALICE. Do I come back?

RACHEL. No.

ALICE. Okay.

She picks up her things, she walks out of the room.

Um. I'm not upset. Okay? Don't worry. I'll see you when you're better… Okay? And maybe we can talk. Okay?

ALICE exits. We hear the clatter of her going down the stairs. ALICE's heels sound more aggressive now.

RACHEL sits in silence, she scratches her eyelid.

Blackout.

3.4

28th February.

ANGELA has partially lifted up RACHEL, and RACHEL is also getting leverage by the use of her arms. ANGELA is pulling the sheet from under RACHEL. This is a complicated but highly efficient procedure.

RACHEL. Ow –

> *ANGELA lifts RACHEL up some more, but keeps pulling the sheet.*

> That's okay.

ANGELA. Okay.

> *ANGELA starts to put a new sheet on the bed. She does so in silence. This is even more of an effort, RACHEL's bum has to be lifted up while the sheet is shunted underneath her.*

RACHEL. Ow.

> *ANGELA finishes and starts filling up a washing basket with RACHEL's clothes from the floor.*

ANGELA. You're almost out of knickers.

RACHEL. Because most of those are clean…

ANGELA. What?

RACHEL. You're washing clean knickers.

> *ANGELA sniffs a pair that she's just put in the basket, the knickers are dirty and smell. She adds them to the basket, while RACHEL giggles. Pause. ANGELA continues putting washing in the basket, as if she hadn't noticed. Then she stops and looks carefully at her daughter.*

Pause. RACHEL looks carefully back. She wipes her cheek roughly, she's not crying, but her cheeks are hot. She's melting slightly.

> I don't want to be like this…

> *Beat.*

ANGELA (*trying not to rush over*). I know you don't, love…

RACHEL. I… um… I want to be nicer now…

ANGELA. Well, nice isn't so important, but let's get you in the chair, let's be positive…

RACHEL. Not the chair.

ANGELA. The chair will be so useful.

RACHEL. Mum, you're saying the wrong things, okay? I want to be nicer, okay?

Pause.

ANGELA. Okay.

Pause. ANGELA *scratches her ear. Pause.*

Do you want to talk to me?

RACHEL. Not yet. But I will.

ANGELA. That's good. That's a relief.

RACHEL. Don't cry.

ANGELA. No, I won't. I do love you, you know that?

RACHEL. Yes, I know that.

Pause.

ANGELA. Do you want me to phone any of your friends?

RACHEL. Not yet.

ANGELA. Okay. And we'll try the chair eventually, will we?

RACHEL. I want to do that slowly.

ANGELA. Okay.

The doorbell rings.

Good.

RACHEL. Don't make a big deal out of it, okay?

ANGELA. No, I won't, I'm just pleased…

RACHEL. Good. I'm pleased too.

The doorbell rings again. ANGELA *flinches.*

ANGELA. Shall I get that?

RACHEL. Yes.

ANGELA. I am pleased, love, okay?

RACHEL. I'm pleased too.

ANGELA. Okay.

ANGELA *exits. Nothing.*

More nothing.

RACHEL *shifts her shoulder, and tries to make it touch the other side of the bed. We can hear someone walking slowly up the stairs.*

They take ages. RACHEL *starts to try and pull herself up the bed. She gets her muscles in a tangle, she gets caught with her right arm acting as pivot at a funny angle.*

JAMES *enters the room.*

JAMES. Your mum let me up…

RACHEL. Okay.

JAMES. Yeah. She seemed really pleased to see me actually. I mean…

RACHEL. Can you just – I need a hand – will you –

JAMES *leans over and supports her back.* RACHEL *readjusts her arm. She's comfortable.*

JAMES (*with one of his smiles*). Hi.

Blackout.

ACT FOUR

4.1

6th March.

She's asleep. PETER *stands about five metres from her bed. He makes as if to move, to sit down. But changes his mind and just remains standing proud.*

He doesn't say anything.

Pause.

PETER. Rach?

> *He sits down, and then stands up again, and moves backwards from the bed.*
>
> *Pause. He notices the wheelchair and walks over and touches it. He then turns away from it as if spotted. He is prowling.*
>
> *He takes off his jumper, he struggles with it slightly.*

Rachel... Rach?

RACHEL (*growling with post-sleep*). Con...

PETER. Hi.

> *Pause. She registers him, she pulls back.*

Hi. I, uh, I'm –

> *Pause. She tries to shift away from him. She's still slightly asleep.*

Hi. Rachel?

> *Pause.*

I just really wanted... to talk to you. Your mum's making dinner, so I thought... you'd need to be awake in a bit, if you like... Do you still want that bed bath? I thought it'd be good to wash – (*Half-laugh.*) before dinner.

> *Pause. He scratches himself and waits. She turns and looks at him.*

Hi.

RACHEL. Okay.

Pause. RACHEL *tries to sit up, he moves as if to help her, but she knows what she's doing now. She puts a pillow from her head underneath her back. Then she pulls herself up using hands on the bedboard, the pillow getting lower and lower down her back as she does. Finally she's in semi-sitting position.* PETER *watches this in awed silence.*

Pause. She looks at him carefully, he looks back.

PETER. Oh. I saw the maddest thing… I was walking, when I was going… home… A man was sitting in his car, listening to his radio. It wasn't that strange. But he looked pretty intense. I thought he was probably listening to the football or something, or he'd had an argument and gone outside to sit in the car. I don't know, but it felt really strange. And then I got scared he was gassing himself, and that I didn't notice, so I went back to check, and he noticed I was checking and smiled at me. It wasn't that mad, it felt pretty strange. He was probably listening to the football.

Pause.

And I've given up the football team… county, I mean… Baylis was really pissed off – 'the first school representative for years' – but it was making me feel too important.

RACHEL (*quiet*). Where have you been?

PETER. I don't know. Listen. Can I do anything? I mean, it doesn't have to be –

RACHEL. Okay. (*Beat.*) You need to buy me some tampons.

PETER. Okay.

RACHEL. I just don't want to ask Mum. She'll just fuss, she got me some last week, but I'm…

PETER. I'll get them. Is there a particular sort? Or…

RACHEL. Whatever's cheapest. Heavy flow.

PETER. Heavy flow, okay.

RACHEL. Take the money out of my top drawer?

PETER. No. I can get it.

RACHEL. Peter –

PETER. No. I've got it. Is there any particular – brand – you prefer?

RACHEL. You want to buy me tampons as a present?

PETER. No.

RACHEL *begins to giggle,* PETER *joins in. She then stops, and looks careful again.*

I'm just pleased you want me back. To give them to you…

RACHEL. Arsched said to say like you weren't coming back – think like –

PETER. Well, he was wrong. I want to be back –

RACHEL. Why?

PETER. Because I want to be… I think that's a pretty good reason…

Pause. RACHEL *shifts her bum slightly, using her hands,* PETER *notices.*

Is it urgent? Do you want me to get them now?

RACHEL. Yeah. I'm bleeding all over the bed.

Pause. He moves his foot and then regrets it.

PETER. Your mum seemed pleased to see me. Though you've been talking, the two of you, yeah?

RACHEL. Did you know James came round?

PETER. Yeah?

RACHEL. He said you hadn't been in school… for a while.

PETER. No.

RACHEL. He asked whether he could do anything. I said, 'How's Alice?' and he got really defensive about that because I'd been a bitch to her when she came round – I said I thought you fancied her and he laughed.

PETER. No.

RACHEL. He said that he'd told you that we hadn't been together long enough for all this – effort –

Pause.

He said he'd said to you he didn't think I was worth it – all this trouble, all this effort and stuff you're doing. He said he didn't want you doing it all just because you felt you had to or because you felt sorry for me and that he had told you that, and that it was unfair of me to expect so much of you. Because it wasn't your fault I'm like this. You weren't doing enough other stuff, other than me, I was basically sort of eating you up. He said he wasn't going behind my back, he wasn't that kind of guy, anything he said to you about me,

he wanted to say to my face as well. So he did – he came
round to see me just so he wasn't talking behind my back.
Which is quite an effort, just so you aren't talking behind
someone's back. You're his best friend so he felt he should
stick up for you, or help you, or say things to me about you
– um… I think he was quite worried about you – being
missing. So, anyway, that was all funny – considering what
I know about him and Alice. Do you think there's
something wrong with him and Alice? Because I do.
Anyway, I thought it was quite brave of him. Though I can't
stand up so…

PETER (*close*). He shouldn't have said that.

RACHEL. Was that what you were thinking? Were you –

PETER. No. No. I mean, we're not that – we're not that – close –
any more –

RACHEL (*soft, quick*). Me and you?

PETER. No. No. James.

RACHEL. Is Alice the reason you argued?

PETER. No. You. Listen, what he said –

RACHEL. She likes you, I think – James is quite rough. Some of
the things she said.

PETER. Yeah? But I'm here with you.

RACHEL. But I think most of the stuff is stuff she does. She
basically tells him to treat her like shit. She's that kind of
girl…

PETER. No. She's not.

RACHEL. Do you fancy her?

PETER. No… I fancy you.

Beat.

RACHEL (*quiet*). Do you want to give me that bed bath?

PETER. Okay.

*Beat. He lets go of her leg. Neither of them look at each
other.*

RACHEL (*nervous, but with a brilliant face on it*). You need to
go and get a – there's a basin in the bathroom with a sponge
in it and some special soap, fill that up, fill it in the bath, or
using the shower otherwise it'll take ages –

PETER. Okay.

He hesitates and then exits, RACHEL *waits.*

She doesn't try and do anything, she just waits, steely-eyed.

Pause. She scratches her nose, touches her scar, smells her hand.

Pause.

Finally, PETER *re-enters, clutching the basin, careful not to spill it.*

RACHEL. Put it on the floor.

PETER. Okay.

RACHEL. Have you put the soap in the water?

PETER. I wasn't sure to – before I poured it – you said it was special soap so…

RACHEL. Put some in now, it's fine.

PETER. I could do it again.

RACHEL. No. Don't.

Beat. PETER *adds soap to the water, and then swirls it round.*

Get the sponge wet.

PETER *does.*

Really squeeze it out, as much as you can.

PETER. Okay.

RACHEL. Now just sponge me down…

PETER. You don't just want to do it yourself…

Beat. She undoes her straps, ready for the top to be taken off. He watches.

RACHEL. I could do my front if you want…

PETER. Okay.

RACHEL (*forced giggle*). But that's the best bit…

PETER. No. You can do it.

RACHEL. I want you to do it.

PETER. Can I do your back first?

RACHEL. Yeah. Help me turn.

He helps her. Then he starts to wipe her back carefully with the cloth. He does so very methodically, lifting up her arms and her hair to get to the places where he thinks she needs cleaning.

Alice likes you, I think, James is quite… rough. Some of the things she said.

PETER. Yeah?

RACHEL. But I think most of it is stuff she does. She basically tells him to treat her like shit, she's that kind of girl…

PETER. I think that's… done.

RACHEL. Turn me over then.

With his help, she turns over onto her front. She makes to cover her breasts, but then changes her mind and makes them as exposed as possible.

PETER. You don't need your face…

RACHEL. No.

He carefully wipes down her body, they hardly breathe. He eventually finishes, he's being so careful, it's beautiful. He finishes and they sit in silence.

PETER. We should get you walking after this…

RACHEL. I've got a wheelchair now.

PETER. Yeah. I saw, I thought that was… great.

Beat. PETER gingerly moves forward and puts RACHEL's straps back on, he hides her breasts for her. She lets him.

RACHEL. What did you really do? When you weren't in school.

PETER. Oh. Um. Walked about. There was a pub where I played the slots a bit. I lost a bit. But… I just walked about mostly, went into shops. But, uh…

RACHEL. Why did you put my straps back on?

PETER. I don't know.

RACHEL. Okay. Now you need to do the bottom half.

PETER. I know.

Pause. They just look at each other.

RACHEL. There's no. Blood.

PETER. Yeah, okay…

RACHEL. Help me turn over again…

PETER. Okay.

He tries to help her turn over, but doesn't want to put much effort into it.

RACHEL. Peter –

He tries again, this time, she turns easily. He lifts up her gown, she pulls her knickers down to her mid-thighs and he, thinking it's a hint, pulls them all the way off and places them beside her on the bed. She says nothing and he starts slowly to clean her. Very, very gently. Then, after he finishes that side, he wordlessly half-lifts her and pulls her back onto her front and then cleans her some more, going all the way down to her feet, he spends a lot of time on her feet. Then he finishes.

PETER. Done.

RACHEL. Okay, just, uh, go to the bathroom and pour it all away. Just leave it how you found it.

PETER. Who did you last time?

RACHEL. The nurse did me a couple of times, then my mum…

PETER. Okay.

He picks up the basin and exits. RACHEL pulls herself down in the bed, so she's back in a lying position. She checks her body, all over, with her hand. PETER re-enters.

RACHEL. Sit on the bed, would you?

PETER. I don't…

RACHEL. Lie down, with me, please…

PETER hesitates, then gets on the bed.

I want to be facing you…

PETER. Okay.

PETER turns her, helps her turn, and then lies down beside her, so that the two of them are facing each other, she strokes his face.

RACHEL. Can I tell you something –

PETER. Yeah.

RACHEL. I followed him because I was scared –

PETER. No. I didn't mean that… question. It wasn't a question.

RACHEL. But I don't want those questions with you –

PETER. I know.

RACHEL. When they first did the photofit – he looked like my dad.

PETER. Oh.

RACHEL. I couldn't get it right. (*Laugh.*) The police wanted to talk to him until they found out... he was dead.

PETER. Okay.

RACHEL. When they showed me the photofit – they said – does that remind you of anyone and I said, 'Yes,' because I realised and they said, 'Who?' And I said, 'That reminds me of my dad.' So they just said, 'Is your dad still at home with you? Billy, can you call the Social in?' And I said, 'My dad's dead,' and I saw Billy – the one they call Billy, I didn't really know him – almost laugh. Because it was quite funny. So I smiled at him, and he just tried to stop laughing, I mean, he didn't let it out. They were really disappointed. And I didn't want you there, to see that, or... anything. I was rubbish at it.

Beat.

Take off your top.

PETER. Now?

RACHEL. I like your chest.

He takes off his top, he struggles a bit. It's difficult taking off your top when you're lying down.

I followed him because I thought if I did anything else then he'd be worse and I didn't put up much of a fight the rest of the time either. And I – when I talked about that stuff, with Arsched, the police, the doctors – I didn't want you there because I was ashamed and I was bad at it. Peter, I couldn't even tell them what he looked like – so / I made him look like my dad...

PETER. I knew that. I wasn't –

RACHEL. Do you mind if I undo my straps? I want to feel me and you...

PETER. Okay.

She undoes her straps halfway.

RACHEL. I don't want to have sex.

PETER. No.

RACHEL. It's okay. I'm still not... ready.

PETER. Yeah.

RACHEL. Okay.

> *Pause, she undoes the remainder of her straps. Then they lie there, in an odd but perfectly formed shape. They try not to breathe.*

> (*Soft.*) I don't think I'd be able to... feel it... anyway... sometimes I can feel it though, when I pee... so...

PETER. Yeah?

RACHEL. But I don't think I'd feel it and that would be...

PETER. Yeah.

RACHEL. When it's our first time, I want it to be about us... Not... I don't want things left to chance.

PETER. No. I'm not – ready – either...

> *Pause.* PETER *clears his throat.*

RACHEL. I'm sorry you won't be... first.

PETER. No. That's okay.

RACHEL. This feels amazing.

PETER. Yeah.

RACHEL. I love you.

> *Beat.*

> Will you take your trousers off...

PETER. I'm...

RACHEL. That's okay, I'm expecting it.

> PETER *does. This takes him a minute, he's not sure how to do it.*

> Will you help me take everything off...

PETER. Okay.

> *They pull her nightie over her head, there's a brief moment of tangle, but then it's all okay.*

RACHEL. This feels amazing, doesn't it?

PETER. I love you too.

RACHEL. Okay.

Beat.

PETER. Are you okay?

RACHEL. No. This is good for me. I think. This is –

PETER. Are you, uh…

RACHEL. I think I can feel you, in my legs, I think I can feel your legs.

PETER. Can you?

RACHEL. Do you want to take your boxer shorts off?

PETER. No.

RACHEL. Okay. Kiss me.

He does. She ventures a hand down his body.

PETER. No. Don't.

RACHEL. It's just a hand.

PETER. No. Don't.

They lie together forever. The Archers *theme music starts playing from downstairs,* RACHEL *giggles through her snot.*

Pause.

(*Soft.*) Are you – crying?

RACHEL. This is better. We'll stay like this – okay?

PETER. Yeah.

RACHEL. It'll be worth it soon – I'll let you – we can make love –

PETER. No. That's not important –

RACHEL. Well, now you know anyway –

PETER. No –

RACHEL. Cuddle me – now you know –

PETER. Okay.

RACHEL. Tighter –

PETER. Okay…

RACHEL. I love you.

PETER. I love you too.

Long pause. She tries to feel closer to him.

RACHEL. I want to turn over, I want you around me, is that okay? I want you tucked up into me. I don't mind. If I can feel anything... I don't mind that...

Beat.

PETER. Okay.

He effects some of this, their bodies spoon. He tries to hold his groin as far away from her as possible. That's an almost impossible task. She tries to nestle in. Then tries again. Then tries a third time. She looks confused, and then upset.

RACHEL. This feels nice.

PETER. Yeah.

She nestles in a fourth time. Moving her back down to him.

RACHEL. You're not...

PETER. No. Not yet.

RACHEL. It's gone down?

Pause. PETER *tries again to move away from her, but there's no room for that.* RACHEL's *perma-smile fades.*

I was just expecting it...

PETER. Yeah?

RACHEL (*soft*). It wasn't something... I did?

PETER. No.

Pause. She picks up his forearm and studies it, he tries to lean over her to see what she's doing, but he can't. Again, it's difficult him being on the bed.

RACHEL (*small*). You do still fancy me?

PETER. Yeah.

She traces a few of the lines on his hand.

RACHEL. I know I don't look amazing... but... It doesn't matter. We can be friends.

PETER. No, we're – you're my girlfriend.

RACHEL (*perfectly soft*). Has anyone tried anything?

PETER. What?

RACHEL. Any of the other girls? Libby? Nicky? Ruth?

PETER. No.

RACHEL (*a delicious forced giggle*). They will. You're quite
fanciable really. I should do an erection test. Say their name,
describe what they look like, and I know them naked, see if
you get one... Libby – let's see – at a guess, 32C – big, long
nipples, she walks around naked in the girl's dressing rooms,
though her arse is bigger than you'd expect. She tried to shave
herself once, and cut it... Alice, short stubby nipples, no
room, Libby's spread out, hers don't... this stomach which tips
slightly over her knickers, not fat, muscle... this perfect arse...

They both stiffen.

Okay. That's okay.

PETER. I'm getting off the bed.

RACHEL. No! DON'T! No!

He half-falls and half-dismounts the bed.

Pause. He's trying to hold in his erection.

PETER. Sorry.

Pause. She isn't sure what to do.

RACHEL. Do you want a blow job? I think I could do one of
those. Do you? You'll have to come closer.

Pause.

I don't mind, Peter. Honestly.

PETER. No.

*Pause. He starts to shuffle back away from her, and then
stops. They stand there for ages.*

Listen – (*Soft.*) Do you really think I can help?

RACHEL. Help what?

PETER. You.

RACHEL. You're supposed to want to see me.

PETER. Yeah?

RACHEL. I think I understand why you're going better than
you do.

PETER. No, I'm not... leaving...

Pause. RACHEL *touches her scar.*

RACHEL. You should stop being friends with James –

PETER. I know.

RACHEL. But don't… Alice – don't rescue her – because she doesn't need it – that's just the way she is – girly, she's not really worth much… She enjoys being a victim too much. Plastic.

PETER. That wasn't Alice, the erection, it wasn't you talking about Alice. It was you, I mean, lying with you, and you kept sticking your bum harder into me when you were telling me about how… I mean, you could have been talking about anyone naked, it was really nice… and just so, with your bum sticking into me. I think you're really pretty, and it was you that gave me the… I'm not put off, and no one… That's what my mum thought, but that's not what…

RACHEL. Okay. Thanks.

PETER. No. No. Don't say thanks.

Pause. RACHEL's shoulders slump, gradually and completely. Until there's almost nothing left.

RACHEL (*slow and soft*). I… I never really liked it when you were here – we always got it wrong, didn't we? I liked you visiting for the bits in between – the bits when you weren't here – when I could dream or plan your next visit – when I could – you're really good to dream about, Peter, you're that kind of person. So it didn't matter when your visits were shit because they were only two or three hours long – or one hour sometimes – and there were twenty or thirty or forty hours in between your visits and I used to just think about you – about how we'd get it right next time. You filled up my brain – and that was – great – when I was just waiting – to get better. Even when you weren't here for thirty days – you filled up my… So – thank you – I'm really grateful for that. I liked thinking about you – sometimes I thought the wrong thing but… you were the good bit. Most of the time, you were something good to think about. So don't be hard on yourself, okay? You did really well.

Beat. He moves his body as if to sit on the bed. But he doesn't move his feet.

But the thing is… I think maybe, if I'm going to get better – I'm going to have to do it without all this… effort. I just want to make everything normal. I'm not sure you can be… make me normal – I'm not sure the effort you make me… is the right kind. I am really grateful though…

Pause.

Did you ever even want to be here?

PETER (*careful, in case he gets the words wrong*). I want to be here now.

Beat. She turns some of her body away from him.

RACHEL (*tired*). Okay.

The lights slowly fade, PETER *just stands there, in his boxers, unsure whether to put his clothes on again or not.*

Blackout.

Music: 'If You Could See Her' from Cabaret.

The End.

Performing Rights

Publication of *A Bed of Roses* and *When You Cure Me* in this book does not necessarily indicate their availability for performance. No performance of any kind may be given unless a licence has been obtained. Applications should be made before rehearsals begin.

Amateur Performing Rights

Applications for performance, including readings and excerpts, by amateurs in English, should be addressed to the Performing Rights Manager, Nick Hern Books, 14 Larden Road, London W3 7ST, *tel* +44 (0)20 8749 4953, *e-mail* info@nickhernbooks.demon.co.uk, except as follows:

Australia: Dominie Drama, 8 Cross Street, Brookvale 2100, *fax* (2) 9938 8695, *e-mail* drama@dominie.com.au

New Zealand: Play Bureau, PO Box 420, New Plymouth, *fax* (6) 753 2150, *e-mail* play.bureau.nz@xtra.co.nz

South Africa: DALRO (pty) Ltd, PO Box 31627, 2017 Braamfontein, *tel* (11) 712 8000, *fax* (11) 403 9094, *e-mail* theatricals@dalro.co.za

United States of America and Canada:
A Bed of Roses: amateur and stock performing rights, contact Nick Hern Books, as above
When You Cure Me: Casarotto Ramsay and Associates Ltd, as below

Professional Performing Rights

Applications for performance by professionals in any medium and in any language throughout the world should be addressed to:

A Bed of Roses: Wintersons, 59 St Martin's Lane, London WC2N 4JS, *tel* +44 (0)20 7836 7849, *e-mail* info@nikiwinterson.com

When You Cure Me: Casarotto Ramsay and Associates Ltd, Waverley House, 7–12 Noel Street, London W1F 8GQ, *fax* +44 (0)20 7287 9128, *e-mail* agents@casarotto.co.uk

WINNER of the THEATRE BOOK PRIZE

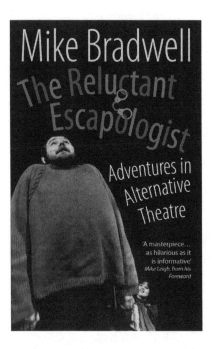

An unrivalled unofficial history of the rise – and partial fall – of fringe theatre, Mike Bradwell's deadpan account of his adventures is one of the funniest and angriest books to come out of theatre today.

'Towards the end of this brilliant account of his epic forty-year journey, Mike tells us, "I don't believe that theatre is safe in the hands of grown-ups", and it is his healthy, eternal youthfulness that makes the book so inspiring' Mike Leigh, from his Foreword

'Inimitably filthy, achingly funny... Bradwell is one of the most colourful figures in theatre today' Ian Herbert, *The Stage*

'Both a history and a pointer to the future of theatre, written by one of its most courageous and effective champions' *Theatres Magazine*

Order from www.nickhernbooks.co.uk